The Tabernacle

Wayne Spence

Printed in the United States of America

First Printing, 2015

ISBN-13: 978-1542524742

ISBN-10: 1542524741

Other Books by Robert Wayne Spence

The Gospel's Sake- 2015
(Available at Amazon)

Who's Watching the Master's Sheep- 2015, 2017
(Available at Amazon)

The Flower Comes Before the Fruit- 2015, 2017
(Available at Amazon)

Acknowledgments

I would like to once again thank all of those that have helped to make another book possible. My wife is always there as a blunt and vocal instrument of correction and guidance. I tend to drift off into areas that have no bearing on the topic of the book or into areas that I may not wish to enter at that point. My philosophy is to be well prepared before jumping into anything else you sink and drown.

I would also like to thank the ministry that contributed to my knowledge base on the Tabernacle. Bible reading and research are major portions of a person's knowledge, yet the ministry has a tremendous effect on it also. Thank each of you so much.

I thank the Lord for every book that He enables me to complete. Without His mercy and grace, I would still be lost in sin and have little to no understanding of the Bible. By His guidance, I find myself authoring my fourth book and I pray it is blessing to Kingdom of God!

Introduction

Jeremiah 30:2 *Thus speaketh the LORD God of Israel, saying, Write thee all the words that I have spoken unto thee in a book.*

After completing my third book, *The Flower Comes Before the Fruit,* I struggled to find direction on what I should focus on for my next book. I had several directions that I felt like I could go but I could never get confirmation from the Lord on which to follow. However, a recent opportunity came my way that pointed me in the direction for this book.

I was approached by a saint in the church and asked to do a lesson on the Tabernacle. I had taught a lesson before in which I touched on the Tabernacle and this saint remembered that and brought it back to my attention. I agreed to do the lesson in a small group setting with the new converts that were struggling with understanding what they were reading in their Bibles.

We met on a Saturday and I explained that it was an informal setting where queries were allowed at any time on anything. The lesson was a success. There were many questions presented that we discussed and sought answers to. After seeing what a need there was for this knowledge (that I had obtained through the teaching of Brother Coon and much personal research) I felt that I should put it in a book. So I am.

This book is meant to be a beginner to intermediate level study in which those unfamiliar with the Tabernacle can acquire a better understanding. The concepts covered, while probing to some intermediate levels, will generally be discussed on an unsophisticated level. There are other authors that conceivably touch a much deeper depth than will be presented here, but hopefully this book will permit anyone with the Holy Ghost a richer understanding of the subjects covered by the simplicity of the presentation.

Chapter 1

Genesis 1:1	*In the beginning God created the heaven and the earth.*
Exodus 33:5	*For the LORD had said unto Moses, Say unto the children of Israel, Ye are a stiffnecked people: I will come up into the midst of thee in a moment, and consume thee: therefore now put off thy ornaments from thee, that I may know what to do unto thee.*

To begin the study of the Tabernacle, one must first understand why man needed the Tabernacle. Why did God require the Tabernacle? What was its significance? Does it apply to the church today? These and other questions will be covered in this book.

To understand why the Tabernacle was needed, it is necessary to go back to the beginning. In the beginning, God created all things along with man. Man, was placed in the Garden of Eden and later a woman was formed for man. During this time, God and man enjoyed a close personal relationship where God would come down each day and walk with Adam. I am sure it was an experience that we cannot even come close to imagining.

Then a problem arose. God had commanded Adam not to eat the fruit of the tree of the knowledge of good and evil. However, Eve was tricked by the serpent into consuming the fruit and she in turn persuaded Adam to eat also. This simple act introduced the sin of disobedience into the life of man and drove a wedge between him and God.

When God arrived to walk with Adam that day, it was revealed that man had sinned so God cast them out of the garden and cursed the woman, the man, and the ground. From this point forward that unadulterated relationship that God had enjoyed with man was destroyed. Now there was a wall between man and God, and that wall was sin. God no longer walked with man as before.

As the reader progresses through the book of Genesis, God warns Noah of the impending destruction to come. However, even though Noah found grace in the sight of God and He warned Noah of the coming flood, that relationship between man and God was still not there. Farther in Genesis the reader finds that God communes with Abraham, who He calls His friend, and they do form a relationship of sorts. Yet that original relationship where God walked with man was still absent.

Then the reader gets to the book of Exodus, and here is found a strong relationship being formed between Moses and God. God speaks to Moses, performs miracles through him, and then uses him to lead Israel out of Egypt. During the journey from Egypt, God leads Israel to Mount Sinai. It is here that the Lord instructs Moses to have the people sanctify themselves and put borders about the mount and then defend those borders.

Why did God do this? Because He is a holy God and there can be no interactions between holy and unholy. The Lord instructs His people to be holy in ***Leviticus 20: 7*** and ***I Peter 1: 15-16***. God will not interact with the unholy and unclean. Look at the following two verses from Haggai:

- ***Haggai 2:12*** *If one bear holy flesh in the skirt of his garment, and with his skirt do touch bread, or pottage, or wine, or oil, or any meat, shall it be holy? And the priests answered and said, No.*
- ***Haggai 2:13*** *Then said Haggai, If one that is unclean by a dead body touch any of these, shall it be unclean? And the priests answered and said, It shall be unclean.*

In these two verses the Lord is showing Israel that touching anything with the holy does not make that which is touched holy. However, touching anything with the unclean does make it unclean. Therefore, the holy and unclean cannot intermingle else all that you have is the unclean.

Based on this premise, it is unimaginable for God, who is holy, to interact with the sinful, the unholy, and the unclean. There must be a separation between the holy and unholy. This was one purpose that the Tabernacle plan was given; so that God could dwell in the midst of the camp of Israel. The other reason was because it was a foreshadowing of the salvation plan.

Figure 1 on the next page is an illustration of the separation of the clean and the unclean. Notice that the Holy only touches the Common and the Clean. The Unclean touches just the Common and the Clean. However, there is no point where the Holy touches the Unclean. This is how it works in God's kingdom.

Figure 1

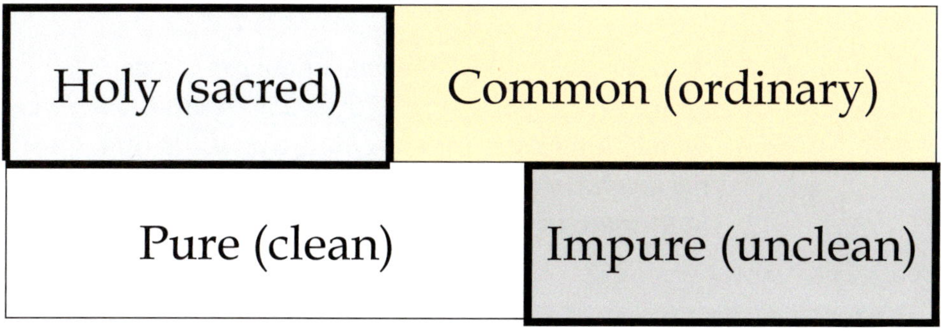

Holy (sacred)	Common (ordinary)
Pure (clean)	Impure (unclean)

Therefore, you can be classified as Holy or common. You can also be classified as clean or unclean. It is possible for a person to be common and clean or common and unclean. On the other hand, a person can only be holy and clean but NEVER holy and unclean. Remember these concepts as the study progresses through the Tabernacle.

Chapter 2

Exodus 38:18 *And the hanging for the gate of the court was needlework, of blue, and purple, and scarlet, and fine twined linen: and twenty cubits was the length, and the height in the breadth was five cubits, answerable to the hangings of the court.*

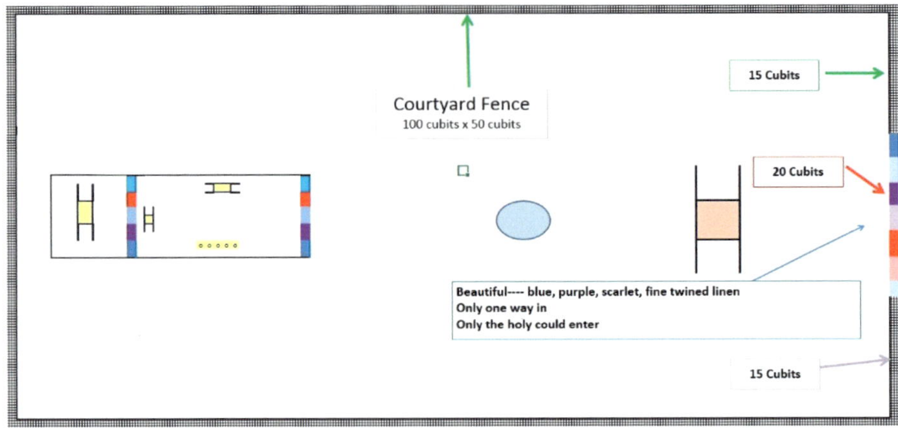

<u>Figure 2</u>- The Courtyard Gate

Scriptures to study on the Courtyard Gate:

Exodus 27: 13-16

Exodus 38: 14-15

When one begins to study the Tabernacle, the first step would be to look at the Courtyard Gate. This would be the first thing that one would encounter as they entered the Tabernacle. If you approach from the north and move in a counterclockwise direction, the only thing you would see before you would be a fence of fine twined linen.

Commentators that I consulted suggest that this would have been a white cloth that stretched around the Courtyard Fence. The height of the fence was five cubits or about seven and a half feet. This is based on a cubit being about eighteen inches in length.

As you make your way around the north side, then the west, then the south, the view would have remained the same. However, as you start around the east side you would see a beautiful work of blue, purple, scarlet, and fine twined linen. This was the Courtyard Gate and it was twenty cubits wide and had four posts which held up this "curtain like" gate.

Scholars suggest that the four posts that held this gate represent the four gospels which provided a gateway from the Old Testament into the New Testament salvation plan. It should be noted also that Jesus stated in ***John 14: 6*** that He was the way, the truth, and the life and that no man comes to the Father but by Him. Therefore, the gate also represents Jesus Christ and the way that He made for man to enter the plan of God.

In addition to these things, the Courtyard Gate would have also been the place where the children of Israel would have brought their sacrifices. There are two schools of thought that I have found on those that entered through this gate. One group believes that the Israelites would have brought their sacrifices through this gate and to the Brazen Altar. The other group believes that only the Priests and Levites could go through this gate. I adopt the belief that only the Priests and Levites could go any further.

One should take note that those that passed through this gate were all dressed alike. God placed guidelines on what was to be worn by those entering the Tabernacle. God also placed many restrictions on who could serve in the Tabernacle. These restrictions may be covered in a future book on the Priesthood. For now, understand that God is concerned with how we dress and what is allowed into the Kingdom.

God did not look at the heart of the priest but rather at their clothing. There are some people that make the statement that God looks on the heart (as mentioned when David was being anointed king) and not on the outside. To put the scripture in its context, God was providing the criteria for selecting a king and not laying down dress code for the people.

This was after Saul was chosen king and had turned from following God. Everyone thought that he was the perfect king because he was such a fine specimen of manhood. This is the same thing that was happening when seeking Saul's replacement. Those that were there in Jesse's house thought that the manly brothers of David were surely the right one for king. Yet God was showing that it is not the outward (fleshly) part of a man that elevates him with God, but rather the inward (spirit) part of man. It is the Holy Ghost within us that lifts us up to be kings and priests in God's Kingdom and not our flesh. This has nothing to do with what you wear.

Therefore, one should follow all the restrictions that God puts into place and not seek to use one restriction to undo another. To participate in the Tabernacle (the Kingdom of God) you had to follow the guidelines and commandments on dress. To look for a suitable king one must understand that God must raise him up because it is the heart that needs to be examined. This is somewhat synonymous with the calling of men into the ministry. God calls them because He looks at many things that we cannot see. If it was up to man to call men to preach, we might choose the best educated, the best speakers, or the best known. Yet God often times calls the uneducated, poor speaking, little known and turns them into powerful preachers.

With this in mind, understand that the restrictions put in place in the Tabernacle by God were for the separation of the holy and unholy. The unclean is not to be brought into the Tabernacle of God else the Tabernacle be polluted. The sacrifices had to undergo a rigorous inspection by the priests BEFORE it was deemed acceptable and brought to the altar. Based on this argument, if the people only brought their sacrifice to the gate, then only the prefect sacrifice would have been able to progress into the Tabernacle. This would have prevented unclean sacrifices from polluting the Brazen Altar and henceforth polluting everyone and everything that touched it.

As you read the book of ***Exodus*** you will encounter scriptures on each part of the Tabernacle. Some may get confused when they discover that these scriptures occur twice. This is because in one instance the pattern is being laid out for the Tabernacle plan. In the next occurrence, the Tabernacle is being described as it is built for the reader to compare what was built with what was planned.

While we will not cover it in this book, let me also point out that there was even order in the placement of the camp. Just as God had guidelines on how the people were to dress, what a perfect sacrifice was, who could enter the Tabernacle; He also had guidelines for where the people camped. The figure below outlines the placement of each of the tribes of Israel.

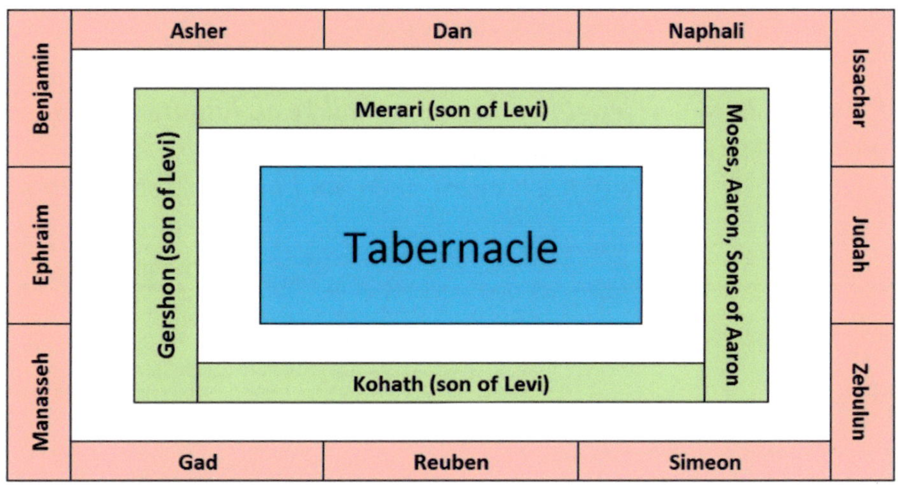

<u>Figure 3</u>- Arrangement of the Camp of Israel

Therefore, the Tabernacle had the Tribe of Levi surrounding it and then the rest of the tribes were placed in an order around them. God was in command of the layout of this Old Testament Tabernacle and He is also in command of the layout of His New Testament Church. To deviate from His plan is to no longer be a part of His plan. There are many churches today that have abandoned God's plan for the church and adopted their own plan. Man's plan leads to sure destruction whereas God's plan leads to sure salvation. We had better stick with the plan of God!

Chapter 3

Exodus 27:18 *The length of the court shall be an hundred cubits, and the breadth fifty every where, and the height five cubits of fine twined linen, and their sockets of brass.*

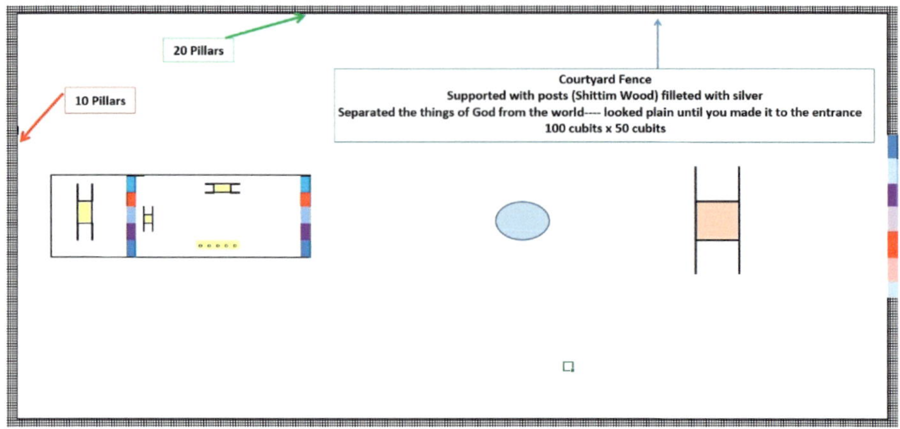

Figure 4- The Courtyard Fence

Scriptures to study on the Courtyard Fence:

Exodus 27: 9-12, 17-18

Exodus 38: 9-20

The Courtyard Fence is one of the least talked about parts of the Tabernacle, yet to me it is one of the most important. This was the only part of the Tabernacle that the world could really see and draw near to. The rest of the Tabernacle was accessible only to the priesthood.

The Courtyard Fence was one hundred cubits long, fifty cubits wide, and five cubits high. The structure was composed of Shittim Wood posts which had a silver chapiter on top, a brass socket at the base, and had silver fillets (rails) and silver hooks attached. Hanging on the silver hooks was the fine twined linen mentioned previously. This fence is depicted in some drawings with the posts visible to the outside and others show the posts visible to the inside. There are even illustrations of the posts as being brass themselves while others reveal the Shittim Wood. I personally believe the posts were visible to the outside and the posts were made of Shittim Wood which I will discuss as I cover this section.

There were four materials used in the construction of the fence. These were the fine twined linen, the silver, the brass, and the Shittim wood. It is important to note the meaning of each of these materials before progressing any further.

The fine twined linen was believed to be white and it represented righteousness. It can be taken considering the other components used in the fence that this was the righteousness of the saints. The white color represents purity and without sin. ***Isaiah 64: 6*** speaks of our righteousness being as filthy rags. Therefore, in order for our righteousness to be pure, there has to be something influencing it.

The silver represents the price for sinner's redemption. This is based on Judas selling Jesus Christ to the priests for silver. This in turn led to Calvary and the purchasing of the new covenant which entitles to all that will, everlasting life. Therefore, it is plain to see that our sinless righteousness hangs on the silver hooks of redemption. The silver fillets are also what holds the components of the fence together.

The brass represents judgment. The brass in the fence is found as sockets, or bases, for the posts. This is always there at the foundation of each post. Man, is due to face the judgment one day for all his sins. Yet, Christ built a way of escape on top of that certain destiny of man. That way of escape is the church and the gospel message.

The final item in the fence is the Shittim Wood posts. The Shittim Wood represents holiness and separation. In the fence this is presented as rigid post that are placed between the holy things of God and the world. We can view these as our standards of separation and holiness.

With the meanings above revealed to the reader, I would like to call attention to a few things. Note that the fine twined linen (the righteousness of the saints) hangs on the silver hooks (price of redemption), which themselves hang on the Shittim Wood posts (separation). Now many churches are throwing away their standards of holiness and separation from the world and embracing worldliness. They are attempting to eliminate "burdens" so that people will be more likely to join their church and feel more comfortable there.

In other words, they are removing the posts from their fence. When the Shittim Wood posts are removed from the Courtyard Fence, the silver is left nothing to attach to. This would cause the silver to fall along with the fine twine linen, or the righteousness of the saints, onto the brass foundation. This would mean that the righteousness of the saints would no longer be spotless, it would no longer be held up by redemption, so it would therefore fall into judgment.

When the posts (separation) of the church starts crumbling and being removed, then that church is removing the structure to which redemption is attached. The holy is being tampered with and that is not acceptable. That leaves the church with nothing but judgment.

The reader needs to be fully aware of the importance of this Courtyard Fence. It was the only thing that separated the holy from the unholy and unclean world. Refer to ***Figure 1*** above to see that the holy and unholy can NEVER intermingle.

When you are studying the Tabernacle please note one very important fact. When the Tabernacle was being assembled the very first time, it was assembled from the inside out. That means that the Ark was anointed and put in its place. The Tabernacle Proper was anointed and erected.

The coverings and the veil were anointed and put in place. All the furniture of the Tabernacle was cleansed, anointed, and put in its place until all that was left to erect was the Courtyard Fence.

At this point, everything else was in its place and was sanctified and holy, yet the Lord did not enter the Tabernacle. However, once the Courtyard Fence was erected, and that separation of the holy from the unholy was in place, THEN the Lord came down into the Tabernacle. Separation matters! Without holiness, no man shall see the Lord. This is especially true in this instance.

When the Lord was ready for Israel to move, they would have to disassemble the camp. Before any part of the Courtyard Fence was taken down the Lord departed from the midst of the Tabernacle. It was this action that let the children of Israel know that it was time to move.

I believe this is what happens in churches that start taking down their stand on holiness. When they start walking toward their fence to remove the first post, I believe that the Lord removes Himself from that congregation. Just as the cloud hovered over the camp to allow them to follow Him, I am sure that the Lord remains over that church that is departing truth. He is there waiting for them to erect again the Tabernacle according to the pattern He provided before He comes back into their midst.

Don't be led astray though by those churches appearing to still be God's church but have lowered their standards. Think back to the erecting of the Tabernacle mentioned above. Before the Courtyard Fence was set up, everything else was in place. It looked like the Tabernacle yet it was lacking that final component needed for God to inhabit it. That works in reverse also. When the Tabernacle was to be moved, the Lord departed as they prepared to disassemble it.

Although scripture does not state it, I would imagine that they would cease offering sacrifices on the Brazen Altar. Then they would start packing things away and covering items up to protect them for the move. The Ark would be covered so it was not visible to anyone. Then the Courtyard Fence would most likely begin to come down. Following this, order would keep the holy things separate until they were ready to be moved.

You may be wondering what this has to do with anything. It is the same way today with churches departing from truth. I cannot see an individual, which was totally for truth, just waking up one day and deciding they were going to remove a post (standard) from their fence today. Departure is a process that builds up to the letting down of a church's stand. Somewhere, the pastor, the church, or both started down a path that led to falling away from God.

The Shittim Wood posts would eventually begin to wear and be damaged by worldly influences (heat, cold, and moisture) which would require periodic repairs and inspections. So too are the holiness standards of the church. If they are not revisited and built back up, they can crumble and fall. Therefore, there is no need to preach false doctrine to leave truth and holiness. All you must do is just neglect to teach on something long enough, and it will eventually decay and no longer be a part of your church.

As a church drifts from truth understand that it still looks like a church. If the entire Courtyard Fence was removed, you would still have everything else in the Tabernacle. Looking at modern day churches that would mean that you would still have preaching, singing, praying, shouting, aisle running, and the whole nine yards. Yet remember that the Lord was not in the Tabernacle UNTIL the Courtyard Fence was in place. (**Figure 5** on the next page shows what the modern-day church with no separation would look like.) There may be goosebumps and moves of the Lord in the services, but we had better never start looking at moves of the Lord as confirmation that He is blessing what we are doing. The Bible is the plumb line that we are to line up to; not the number of goosebumps.

Figure 5- The Tabernacle without the Courtyard Fence (The Church of Today- No Separation)

I am probably going to get some push back from the previous paragraph. However, if you think that the goosebumps are a good indication of the approval of God, then why do churches that have left separation still experience it? If we adopt that mindset, then the charismatic churches are in God's will and the emergent church is in God's will. I don't know what the cowboy church and others experience, but if they feel God, then we would have to acknowledge that they are also in God's will if we are going by what I would call the 'goosebump theology'.

I don't buy it. The Bible is very plain about the separation of the holy from the unholy. I am sorry, but churches that allow adultery, fornication, and other sins during the week and come together on Sunday to feel the goosebumps, are NOT separate and holy. The church of the living God should have more wisdom than to follow this foolish theology.

In fact, there are many things that cause goosebumps besides the presence of God. Looking at the physiology behind the phenomenon called goosebumps, we find that this is just a temporary local change in the skin caused by nerve discharges from the Sympathetic Nervous System. This is an involuntary nervous system, which means that we have no control over it. When some type of stimulus is encountered, it causes a nerve discharge which causes contractions of the arrectores pilorum (hair erector muscles) thereby elevating the hair follicles.

This elevating of the hair follicles occurs due to a release of adrenaline which is a stress hormone. There are pleasurable and unpleasurable stresses yet the body is unable to differentiate between the two. In addition to generating goosebumps, the release of the adrenaline can also produce teary eyes, sweaty or trembling hands, increases in blood pressure, increases to heart rate, and butterflies in the stomach.

There are many types of stimulus that may stimulate the formation of goosebumps. Usually they include some type of emotional apex involving feelings such as: fear, surprise, defense, and admiration, feelings of awe, love, grief, excitement, and even patriotism. In addition to these there are a couple of other things that may also produce goosebumps.

One of these things is hearing music. Yes, even music itself may attribute to the forming of goosebumps. Therefore, having the right music program can produce goosebumps in any setting, whether it is of God or not. Another contributor to goosebumps is the reaction to powerful people. This has been linked to seeing powerful people as dangerous. Therefore, a motivational and charismatic speaker can illicit goosebumps from the crowd. Based upon this small look at the ability to produce goosebumps outside of the spiritual, I think it would be foolish to rely on goosebumps as a gauge of how in tune with God and His plan that you are.

Remember even as the Tabernacle was being erected or dismantled, the manna still fell every day from heaven. Just having the components of the Tabernacle in your possession allowed you to partake of that blessing sent down from haven. However, God did not reside IN the camp until the Tabernacle was erected according to the pattern.

The same is true in the church of today. Having all the components in the church required by God allows for the blessings from heaven to fall on you. Yet, if those components are not arranged and managed per God's plan, you just have the manna falling but not God in your midst. This leads churches to justify their departure from truth and holiness and believe that they are blessed of God.

In the New Testament church, it is not God leaving the church, but rather the church leaving God. Remember that backsliding churches were once the sheep of His pasture and He said that He would seek that which was lost. He will come to their services to try and win them back. However, they see that as approval and they never seem to look for a way back to truth. Why go back when you feel that you are saved where you are? You will not.

Let me close this chapter by saying that we MUST have our standards in place. With that said, let me also point out that periodically someone is going to have to inspect those posts and make sure that they are not damaged, not cracking, and not in danger of falling. This MUST be done by the pastor through teaching his church separation and holiness. Remember, that each of us have a fence around us to keep us separate from the world.

We are the Tabernacle of God in which He now dwells. Teaching holiness and standards allows every saint to examine their own posts as the pastor is examining those of the church. Now every saint will know where they need to make any necessary repairs to their fencepost and are strengthened in their resolve by the importance placed on the fence by the pastor through his teaching.

The saints pick up on what the pastor feels is important by what he teaches. If a pastor wants holiness in the church, then teach it else it crumbles and depart. If a pastor does not want holiness in their church, then never teach it and eventually you will see holiness slowly depart.

Those that begin to remove the posts from the Courtyard Fence will find that their righteousness has once again become as filthy rags and they have fallen into judgment. It is a fearful thing to think of all the people and churches becoming lax in these last days as they gamble that what they practice is enough to make it to heaven. Oh, what anguish to learn on judgment day that you have missed the mark entirely? Whether you missed it by an inch or a mile is irrelevant in eternity.

However, to face the realization that the removal of that one single post is what cost you eternal life will be a devastating blow. Can we remove any posts and still be saved? If we can remove one and be saved, who knows for sure which one it is? If we could remove ten and still be saved, who knows for sure which ten it is?

I am convinced that we cannot remove any post and make it to Heaven. To remove any post would cause a weakness in the fence and a slackness. Now you have potentially opened a way for the unclean to mix with the clean. The stress on the rest of the fence would likely cause more damage to occur to the point that the fence would soon collapse to the ground. Then ANYTHING could enter and I hope you understand that the holy would depart. "God help us all to see what is happening to the church and turn back to You with our whole hearts", is my prayer.

Chapter 4

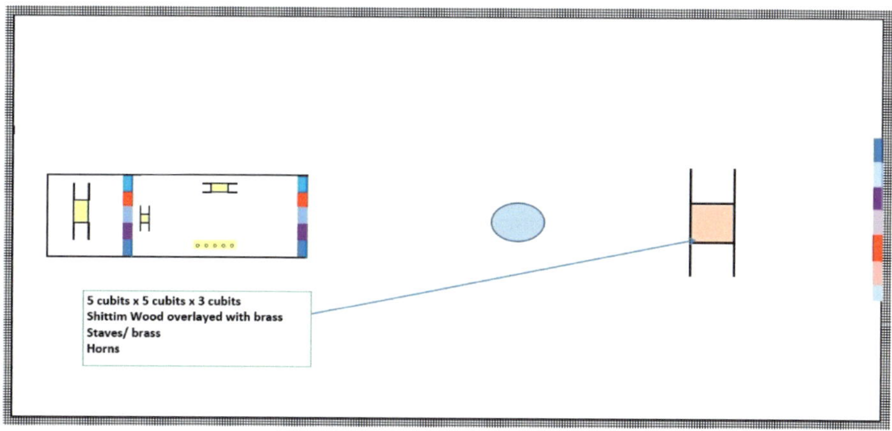

Figure 6- The Brazen Altar

Scriptures to study on the Brazen Altar:

Exodus 27: 1-8

Exodus 38: 1-7

As one entered the Gate of the Courtyard Fence, the first thing encountered would be the Brazen Altar. This structure was five cubits by five cubits by three cubits in height. It was made of Shittim Wood overlaid with brass. There were horns on each corner of the Altar along with four rings for the staves. The staves were made of Shittim Wood overlaid with brass.

The Brazen Altar was the place where sacrifices were offered. This was a place of death and would have maintained an odor of burnt flesh and blood. This would have been a place that would have been repulsive to most people because of the smell, the sound, and the sight.

This place of death and blood represents "repentance" in the New Testament church. Repentance can be viewed as the dying of the "old man" when we lay ourselves on the altar before God. When you become broken in the presence of God and truly repent, you die out to your old way of doing things as you turn toward the things of God.

True repentance carries with it an awesome blessing from God as you throw down your sin and pick up your cross and endeavor to follow Christ. This blessing of repentance is what confuses some people in denominational churches. There are those that believe that what you feel in repentance is actually the infilling of the Holy Ghost. I have even had people tell me that I could "never tell them they didn't experience something" when they went to the altar and repented. I agree. I have experienced what they speak of but I know that there is more to come if you keep on seeking and keep on knocking. It gets much better than that.

I am not sure why there are so many churches and people that reject, or frown on, speaking in tongues. How can you truly be a Christian and not believe the entire Bible? The Bible says that God never changes and we know that His arm is not shortened and He has not lost any power. If it is in the Bible, then we need to explore it.

Remember that the New Testament church was started in the book of ***Acts***. When you read the remainder of the New Testament you are for the most part reading letters to the churches or to ministers in the church. The exception would be the book of ***Revelations*** which is in a class all by itself. Therefore, if you want to know how to get into the church that the apostles started, then you need to go where that church started; the book of ***Acts***.

As you study the book of ***Acts*** you find that the church began with only Jews. There was no desire on anyone's part to include the Gentiles, who were viewed as dogs. So, when Peter was sent to Cornelius in ***Acts*** chapter ten, we have the first Gentiles added to the church. There was a big uproar in the church over this because no one thought Gentiles were to be allowed into the church.

The leaders of the church called Peter before the council to find out what he was thinking when he went to the Gentiles, which was not an acceptable practice for the Jews. Peter explained the vision that God had given him and the instruction from God to go with the men at the front gate. He then described how he followed the men, heard Cornelius's explanation, and then preached Jesus unto them.

At this point, Peter informs the council that while he was preaching, the household of Cornelius received the Holy Ghost. How was he able to convince the council that they really received the Holy Ghost? Was it by saying they experienced something when they repented? No, this requires you to take someone's word that they received the Holy Ghost and the council would not have accepted this explanation.

Yet the council could not deny that the Gentiles were beneficiaries of the Holy Ghost when Peter told them that they all spoke with other tongues as the Spirit gave them utterance. No man can replicate that and those around you can verify it. No need to tell anyone you receive the Holy Ghost when they see and hear for themselves that you spoke in tongues just like the Bible says.

If you have not experienced it, please do not speak against it. At one point, everyone thought the earth was flat; until it was proven that it was round. Spontaneous generation was once thought to be possible until that idea was proven wrong by Pasteur. Consequently, do not discard what the Bible has to say about speaking in tongues. Nevertheless, to receive the Holy Ghost, a person must desire it more than anything else. This excludes many people that want to live as they want and not conform to what God wants. This group will not get the Holy Ghost without a transforming of their mind.

Looking back at the structure of the Brazen Altar, it should be noted that it was three cubits high or about four and a half feet. This is about the level of the sternum on an average size male. Based on this information, it is very evident that lifting a sacrifice onto the Altar would have been a strenuous exercise. Once anyone lifts above about waist height, then you are using almost completely the arms. Therefore, offering sacrifices on the Brazen Altar would not have been an easy task.

The same is true in the church today. When a sinner comes to God, making that first step to the altar is sometimes the most difficult step you will ever make. You are in essence taking yourself (the sacrifice) and placing it on the altar before God. For me, it was the hardest thing I ever did. I was so shy and bashful that when the Holy Ghost would pull at me I would grip the back of the pew before me and squeeze with all the strength I had.

It was like I was being pulled away by an army to my death and I was trying to save myself. That is exactly what was happening I guess. My soul, or inner man, was trying to get to the altar but my flesh was fighting it because that is where the flesh would die. I am so grateful that God made a way for me to get to the altar. At that altar, something died within me, but something was also born within me. A hunger for all God had for me drove me until I received the Holy Ghost. Thank God for making a way.

The final point I would like to make is that the fire on the Brazen Altar was never allowed to be extinguished. That is how the Kingdom of God is also. When you enter the church, you enter by first repenting. However, that is not the only time that you will repent. We are to keep living a repented life because while we do have the Holy Ghost, it is housed in an earthen, fleshly, vessel. That flesh is going to fail often and we will have to come back again to the Altar and repent, thereby keeping the fire going on our Altar.

The horns on the altar represent power. Repentance delivers power to the saint in that it enables them to proceed farther in the Kingdom of God. Therefore, maintaining a life of repentance not only keeps the fire burning on the altar, it also delivers power to the saint of God.

Chapter 5

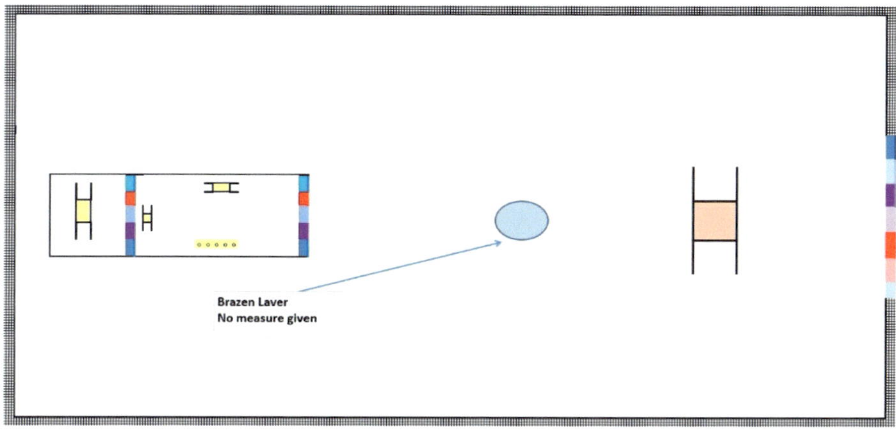

Figure 7- The Brazen Laver

Scriptures to study on the Brazen Laver:

Exodus 30: 18-21

Exodus 38: 8

The Brazen Laver is the next item that would be encountered after you passed the Brazen Altar. There were no measurements given for this structure. It is revealed in the Bible however, that the Laver was constructed from the looking glasses of the women. These looking glasses would be brazen structures polished so smoothly that they acted as mirrors. Commandment was also given that anyone entering the Tabernacle Proper had to first wash their hands and feet in the Laver else they die.

The Laver represented two things. First, it represented baptism. Understand that when the priests finished offering sacrifices on the Altar, they would have to stop and wash their hands in this Laver. Therefore, the blood of the sacrifices found its way into the water of the Laver and then EVERYONE else that washed in the Laver came in contact with the blood. This is what happens in baptism. Jesus Christ was our High Priest (***Hebrews 4:14***), yet He was also the spotless Lamb (sacrifice) of God. To understand fully about the blood in the Laver, we need to look briefly at the Day of Atonement.

The Day of Atonement was the occasion when all the sins of Israel were rolled ahead for one year. This was something the Lord instituted to help deal with the sin issue until Calvary. On the Day of Atonement, the High Priest would offer a bullock for himself and his family on the Brazen Altar. Then he would take of the blood of that sacrifice and he would wash at the Laver. Then enter the Holy Place and go behind the Veil and sprinkle the blood on the Mercy Seat to atone for his sin. Note that this was the only day of the year that ANYONE was allowed behind the Veil.

Once this was completed, the High Priest left the Tabernacle Proper and went to the Tabernacle Gate. There at the gate were two goats that had been chosen for this occasion. They would cast lots to determine which goat would be the sacrifice and which goat would be the scapegoat.

The one chosen to be the scapegoat was brought forth and the elders of Israel laid their hands on its head and confessed all the sins of Israel. Then the goat was led far away from the camp by what the Bible calls a "fit man". It is taught that if that goat returned to the camp then the sins would also return with it. However, if the goat did not return, then the Lord would forget their sins until next year, when they would accumulate again.

The second goat became the sacrifice for Israel. The High Priest would offer this goat on the Brazen Altar, wash at the Laver, and then take its blood into the Tabernacle Proper. He would first place blood on the horns of the Altar of Incense. Next, he would go behind the Veil again where he would sprinkle the blood on the Mercy Seat.

All this information is important to the study of the Laver. Remember that Jesus was the High Priest, the sacrifice, and He was also the scapegoat. He was the scapegoat in that all our sins were laid on Him and He took them away where they will never come back. He was also the fit man that led the sins to a place that they could never return to the camp. ***Psalms 103: 12*** says that "As far as the east is from the west, so far hath he removed our transgressions from us".

Jesus was the sacrifice in that He was the Lamb slain from the foundation of the world (***Revelations 13:8***). He was sacrificed on Calvary that we might have eternal life. His blood was shed for our sins. In addition to this, Jesus is our High Priest as spoke of in ***Hebrews 2: 17, 3: 1, 4: 14-15, 5: 5, 5: 10, 6: 20, 7: 26-28, 8: 1-3, 9: 7-25, 10: 21,*** and ***13: 11***. I encourage you to read the book of Hebrews as you are studying the Tabernacle. It will compliment and shed more light on the topic for you.

Considering all this information, let me break it down for you. Our High Priest (Jesus) offered Himself as a sacrifice whereby He took of His blood, washed in the Laver, then entered the Holy Place and behind the Veil, where He sprinkled the Mercy Seat for our redemption. Another awesome thing is that when you study ***Romans 3: 25*** you find that Jesus became our propitiation, which in the original Greek means mercy seat. Therefore, Jesus became our Mercy Seat also whereby we obtain mercy through Him.

Finally, Jesus acted as that Fit Man. When Jesus ascended into heaven to sprinkle His blood in that heavenly Tabernacle, He took our sins with Him and removed them as far as the east is from the west as stated above. He took our sins to a place that no other person could have taken them.

With all of this in mind, remember that the blood of the sacrifice (Jesus) was placed in the water of baptism when He washed His hands in it as He went in to sprinkle the blood on the Mercy Seat. Therefore, everyone being baptized in the name of Jesus has the blood of "the" sacrifice applied to them. This gives them a clean conscience and allows them to seek for the Holy Ghost (***I Peter 3:21***). Let me also stress here that Jesus only entered the Holy Place once because He did not have to make a sacrifice for himself as the High Priest of the Old Testament did (***Hebrews 7:27***). This was because He was without sin and needed no sacrifice for Himself. The Tabernacle is such a beautiful thing when a person sees what it represents in the Kingdom.

Therefore, the Laver represents baptism. To be more specific, it represents baptism in Jesus name. The Laver also represents one other thing and that is the "washing of water of the word" mentioned in ***Ephesians 5: 26***. This is God's way of cleansing His church so that it can be without spot or blemish.

When you are baptized, you go through a process whereby you examine yourself and see that you are a creature of sin and that you need forgiveness. Remember the Laver was made from the looking glasses of the women. Therefore, when you were washing in the Laver, you could see your reflection in the water. This is what happens when you see your sinful self and are baptized.

This is also what happens when the word is preached in the church. That word goes forth and pricks the heart of those hearing it. This causes one to see themselves in what is being preached and thereby causes them to seek to align with the word. This constant examining of ourselves is how God keeps His church clean. We are in essence washing continuously at the Laver when we see our faults in the word.

Chapter 6

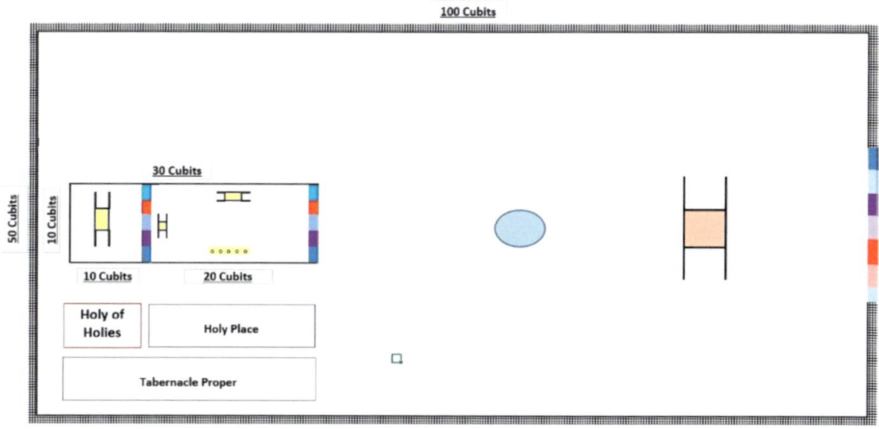

Figure 8- The Tabernacle Proper

Scriptures to study on the Tabernacle Proper:

Exodus 26: 1-29, 36-37

Exodus 36: 37-38

Exodus 38: 8-34

The Tabernacle Proper is everything else inside the Courtyard Fence. That would include the ten cubits by thirty cubits by ten cubits high structure, the coverings, the entrance curtains, the Candlestick, the Altar of Incense, the Table of Shewbread, the Veil, and the Ark. The Tabernacle Proper is broken down into two regions, the Holy Place and the Holy of Holies.

The Holy Place is what one would first enter as you stepped into the Tabernacle Proper. On your right side, would be the Table of Shewbread, on your left side would be the Golden Candlestick, and straight ahead would be the Altar of Incense which sat before the Veil. The three walls of the Tabernacle Proper were made of Shittim Wood and overlaid with gold. These boards sat in silver sockets. Gold is the purity or holiness of man but it rests on the price of redemption (silver).

The Holy of Holies was beyond the Veil. If you walked through the Holy Place, you would reach the Veil. Stepping through this Veil would bring you into the Holy of Holies where sat the Ark of the Covenant with its Mercy Seat. This is the place that the high priest could only enter one day a year, and that was on the Day of Atonement.

The Tabernacle Proper was covered with four different coverings. The inner most covering was of blue, purple, scarlet, and fine twined linen. This is what would have been visible from within the Tabernacle Proper. This represents royalty. The covering that rested on the Fine Twine Linen was the one of goat's hair which would have been white. This represents the righteousness of Christ and of the saints.

The next covering was of ram's skins dyed red. This represents the suffering of Christ and the blood that washed us. The final covering was made of badger's skins. This was what would be visible to the outside world. It represented concealment of divine glory in humility. It could have also represented the outer covering of man, or his flesh.

Therefore, looking at the coverings from outside to inside, there would be the flesh of man that is visible to the world. It would look ordinary and unimportant. However, beneath that would be the blood of Christ that purchased our redemption and washed us. The next layer would be the white (purity) that is made possible by the blood of the Lamb. Finally, the inside is where the Holy Ghost resides, and this is where that our royalty is linked.

The world looks at the saints of God and just see another human being standing there; nothing special. Yet, if they could only look inside of us they would see the beauty and splendor of the Holy Ghost residing in us and our spotless robe of righteousness. This is only made possible by that layer of Lamb's blood applied right below the surface.

Looking back at the Tabernacle in Wilderness, it should be noted that the Tabernacle Proper was ten cubits high while the Courtyard Fence was only five cubits high. This meant that the camp of Israel could see the Tabernacle Proper over the Courtyard Fence. While most of what was visible was just the unattractive badger skins, this was not the case for the entrance to the Tabernacle Proper.

Anyone entering through the gate of the Courtyard Fence would pass by the Brazen Altar, then past the Brazen Laver, and then they would be standing before the only entrance into the Holy Place. This entrance was of blue, purple, scarlet, and fine twined linen. It would have been another beautiful work just as the Courtyard Fence Gate. Therefore, one approaching the Tabernacle from the east would see the Gate of the Courtyard Fence and above it in the distance would be the beautiful entrance to the Holy Place.

This was sure to prick the curiosity of those approaching causing them to desire to see more of that entrance in the distance. This is also how it is when one enters the Kingdom of God. As the preacher begins to deliver the word, he paints the beautiful picture of Jesus and how He died for our sins. Then he goes on to describe how Jesus died for everyone, even you. Now you can see the beautiful Gate in the Courtyard Fence but it is up to you to decide whether to enter or not.

Even as you are beginning to see the beautiful Gate, the preacher goes on and starts talking about the eternal life that was purchased for whosoever will. Now you are presented with not only the forgiveness of your sins right this moment, but also a beautiful picture of the future where you can live forever with Jesus Christ. That futuristic promise is like that

Holy Place entrance you can see in the distance above the Courtyard Fence Gate.

Those that come humbly before the Lord when approaching the Kingdom can only see the fine twined linen of the Fence (righteousness of the saints) and the beauty of the entry. Those are ready for what God has for them. On the other hand, those that approach with a haughty, puffed up, and elevated attitude, find themselves elevated up where they can see the Brazen Altar and the Brazen Laver. They become focused on the sacrifice required and the requirements in place to approach God. This causes them to overlook the beauty and focus on what they feel are undue burdens, so they turn back and do not enter.

Only those that come to God with a humble heart will be able to see the beauty of God's plan. When they are sold on the message, they hunger to step through that Gate of beauty. When they step through the Gate, they are so convinced of the plan that they readily kneel at the Altar and offer themselves a sacrifice. When their sacrifice of repentance is made, then they are ready to proceed to the Laver of baptism and onward to the Holy Place. God's plan is awesome!

Chapter 7

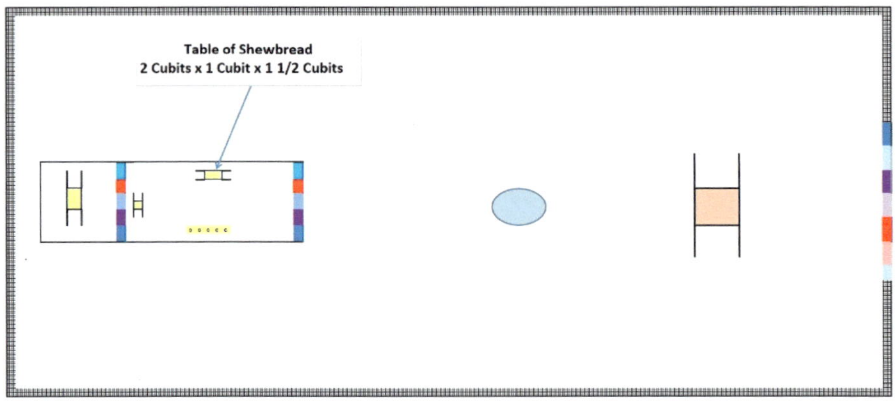

Figure 9- The Table of Shewbread

Scriptures to study on the Table of Shewbread:

Exodus 25: 23-30

Exodus 37: 10-16

As one would step through the entrance of the Holy Place, there would be three pieces of furniture visible. In this chapter, we will focus on the item on the right side, or north side, which would be the Table of Shewbread. Its measurements were two cubits by one cubit by one and a half cubits high. The showbread represented two things. First, it represented Jesus Christ who was the bread sent down from heaven as recorded in ***John 6: 41, 51***. However, it also represented the word of God. The Bible is our daily bread that we take in and live.

The Table of Shewbread was made of Shittim Wood overlaid with pure gold. The Bible specifies some items as having 'gold' while others have 'pure gold'. This is an interesting study that I will touch on later in this book. The Table of Shewbread also had four rings attached to it, one at each corner. Two staves of Shittim Wood overlaid with gold were placed in the rings to carry it.

There was a crown about the top of the table which would prevent anything from falling from the top. Therefore, this would prevent the bread, or the word of God, from falling to the ground. The Lord stated in ***Ezekiel 12: 25*** that He would speak and His word would come to pass. It will not fall to the ground as dead, but will continue until it is fulfilled. Jesus mentioned in ***John 15: 25*** that the word would be fulfilled.

Upon this Table of Shewbread were twelve loaves of bread placed every Sabbath. The twelve loaves represented the twelve tribes of Israel. The loaves were unleavened. Leaven represents sin, so these loaves were without sin. When the new bread was placed on the Table of Shewbread on the Sabbath, the old bread was removed and eaten by the priests. This old bread had sat on the table for seven days and was covered with the incense from the Altar of Incense that was burned twice a day.

This old bread was hallowed, or made holy, by the Lord because it was laid up before Him. This is how it should work in the church today. We are the priesthood (spiritually) and we should be eating the word of God (bread) that has been laid up before Him until it is hallowed. This is that word that has been delivered to us by men of God that fasted and prayed and sought God's will and His truth.

However, as we progress as a movement and new men come on the scene, there is a move toward abandoning the old bread (word) and baking new bread. Ministers are departing from the stands that our elders made, as new 'revelations' and new 'nuggets' are sought. That search for a new nugget for every service requires that the word of God gets stretched further and further to provide new inspirational and inspiring messages.

The desire for the old bread of our elders is diminishing as the ministry tires of the same old stale taste. They want a new and fresh taste to their bread (word/preaching) to move the crowds and attract more people. What they do not understand though is that God only hallowed that bread that was laid up before Him for seven days. Four days, five days, or six days would not do; it had to be seven days. The incense that was on the hallowed bread in the Tabernacle is absent in the new bread offered by many churches today.

Preaching new revelations may be like biting into a fresh piece of bread as opposed to old stale bread, but it is no longer hallowed or holy. This may explain why so many churches are leaving holiness; maybe it is because they are no longer feeding holy bread to their saints. Lord help us!

There is a cry throughout the ministry for revival. What they are talking about is a harvest of new souls. However, what we really need is an old-fashioned revival of desiring the old bread. We need to return to the old paths and what the old preachers stood for.

It is amazing to me that the old bread was embraced by men that fasted and sought God and His will, while the new bread is being sought by men that spend their time in recreation and other pursuits instead of fasting and seeking God. For us to embrace what our elders did, we are going to have to seek God the way they did. Anything less will produce less.

On a final note, the Israelites tired of the manna in the wilderness and influenced their leadership to provide something different. This led to them sinning and having the wrath of God fall on them. We need to support the ministry that still sets the table with the old bread. That is what will save us and our children.

Chapter 8

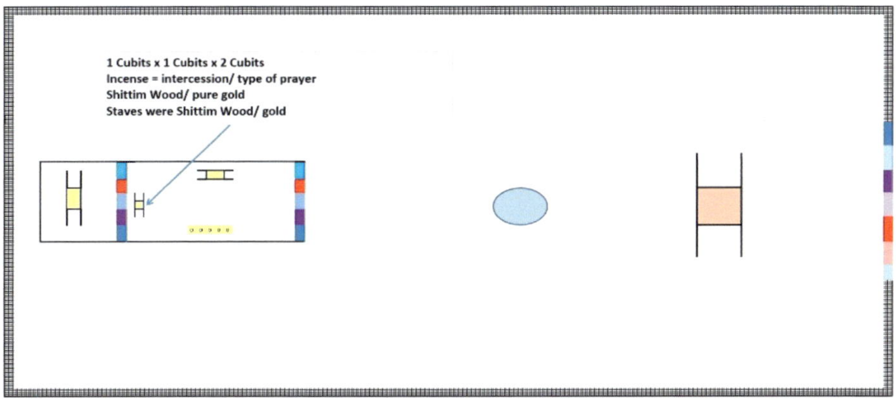

Figure 10- The Altar of Incense

Scriptures to study on the Altar of Incense:

Exodus 30: 1-10

Exodus 37: 25-29

The Altar of Incense was one cubit by one cubit by two cubits high. It was made of Shittim Wood overlaid with pure gold. There were four horns; one on each corner. It had rings of gold into which went the staves of Shittim Wood overlaid with gold. There was also a crown of gold around about the top of it.

The high priest was to go in every morning and burn sweet incense on it (***Exodus 30: 7***) and every evening (***Exodus 30: 8***). There was to be no strange incense placed on it, nor burnt offering, nor meat offering, nor drink offering. This was just a place for the sweet incense.

The incense represents the prayers of the saints. Some commentators also infer that it represents the praise and worship of the saints. It was upon the horns of this Altar that the blood from the Day of Atonement sacrifice was placed and where it remained throughout the year as a remembrance of the mercy of God.

King Uzziah thought to offer incense before the Altar of Incense although he was not of the lineage of Aaron the high priest. The priests withstood him and God smote him with leprosy for his error. So, understand that the ONLY people that can offer incense at this Altar are those that are of the priesthood. In other words, you must be adopted into the family by the infilling of the Holy Ghost. This makes us sons of our High Priest and therefore eligible to offer incense before the Lord.

Note here that this Altar was small. It was only about eighteen inches by eighteen inches. It was not designed for the burning of wood. So, to burn incense the priest would have to bring coals from the Brazen Altar in a censor. Therefore, it was necessary for the Brazen Altar fire to remain burning as the Lord commanded to have access to the hot coals necessary for burning incense.

Saints today must also keep the fires of repentance burning in their lives every day if they are going to be able to offer up incense to the Lord. In other words, we must repent and keep our bodies under subjection to the Lord if we are to have our prayers, praise, and worship rise to the Lord. Without the coals from a repentant life, our incense is just a powder that has no heat to create a sweet savor unto the Lord.

Based on this, it would seem as though the only prayers heard by the Lord are those of the saints. The exception to this would be a sinner's prayer for salvation. This would have to be the case since the only people allowed into the Tabernacle were the priesthood and the only ones allowed to offer incense were the priesthood.

It is interesting, however, that it seems as if the Lord does answer some prayers of people that are not in God's Kingdom. After consideration, I can come to only one conclusion on the matter; prayers of those not of the priesthood (unsaved) that align with the will of the Lord are mistakenly taken as answered prayers. Therefore, a sinner praying for something that is in God's will would see this as their prayer coming to pass. I would argue though, that it is the children of the King that can truly petition the King for their requests. It pays to be a CHILD of the King.

Chapter 9

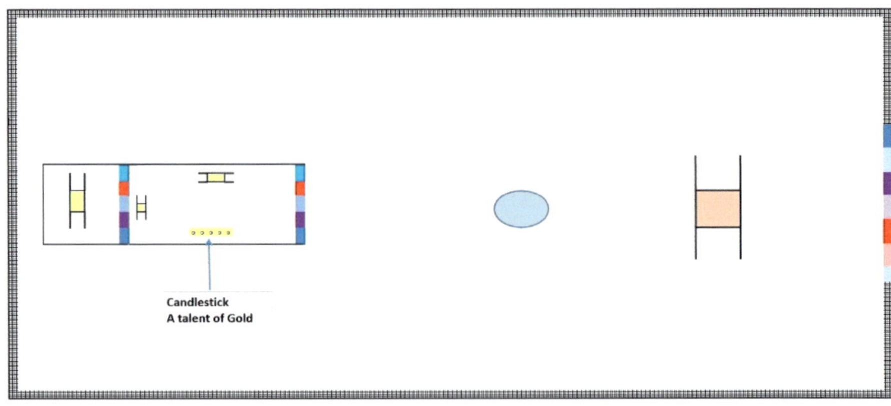

Figure 11- The Candlestick

Scriptures to study on the Candlestick:

Exodus 25: 31-40

Exodus 37: 17-24

The Candlestick was constructed of a talent of pure gold. It was located on the left, or the south side, as one entered the Holy Place. The structure of the candlestick consisted of a main "trunk" and three branches that sprung off both sides. Each of these had a knop and flower, a knop and a flower, a knop and a flower. Each one terminated with a bowl shaped like an almond that contained the oil which was used to provide the light. The Bible records that the Candlestick was a beaten work. This refers to Jesus being beaten and scourged (***Isaiah 52: 14***).

The candlestick provided the only light within the Tabernacle Proper. It represents Jesus as the light of the world and God who is light. There should be no problem accepting this if you realize that God was manifest in the man Christ Jesus. There is only one God. We will save the oneness for another message.

However, when you understand what this represents, then look back at its structure. The knop means "closed" in the original Hebrew. If you take this in addition to the flower and the almond shaped bowl (which held the oil), then it is easy to see that Knop means a closed bud. So, you have a bud, a flower, and then a fruit. Looking at the revelation of the godhead, we have it being hidden in the Old Testament from man's understanding. It was like a closed bud. Then God began to slowly reveal Himself to man.

When the New Testament arrives, we have the bud opening to a flower and the revealing of the invisible God in the visible form of Jesus. Then just as it occurs in nature, the flower died and then the fruit or the oil was available. Once Jesus died we have the Holy Ghost given to man which is the oil. Note that all three of these were represented on one candlestick, not three. Those are not three separate entities, but rather one.

It was the burning of the oil of the candlestick that provided the light. That oil represents the Holy Ghost. The Bible states in ***I John 2: 27*** that the Holy Ghost will teach you all things. Therefore, it gives the light of revelation to the saint of God. Note that the Holy Ghost (that oil) resides within the saint and the saint is like that wick which the oil flows through. When the wick is lit, then the oil is burned and light is made available to the darkness. When the saint gets on fire the Holy Ghost flows through them and is a light of witness and testimony to those in darkness. The "cold" saint sheds no light to those in darkness.

Even a "hot" saint that is burning bright can have issues. When the wick burns for long periods of time, it tends to become less efficient and the light becomes dimmer and smoke begins to be emitted. When this occurs, the light is less visible yet the wick becomes more visible. This same thing can happen with man, when they become so spiritual, or so used, that the focus becomes more on the wick (man) and less of the light (God) is seen. Some of these begin to think that they are in the driver's seat and the Holy Ghost is just following them. Others can get so caught up in themselves to where they begin to try forcing moves of the Spirit when they want it instead of following the leading of the Spirit.

However, if that wick is trimmed, then the light becomes brighter and the wick is more difficult to see.

That is why it was one of the priest's jobs to come in and trim the wick and refill the vessel with oil. This caused the candlestick to keep the light bright and ensure that it did not go out. When the preached word of God goes forth from the pulpit, it is trimming the wick of the saints. It is refilling those vessels with oil so that the fire will not go out. When this trimming and filling takes place, the saints exhibit more of the light (Jesus) and less of themselves (the flesh).

When everything is being performed as it should, then the only light in the church should be Jesus and the light of truth and revelation. The saints should be yielding to the Spirit and not the flesh. However, there were times that the light of the world would be visible inside the Holy Place. This was when someone was entering or leaving.

The same is in the church today. The light of the world should have no place in the church unless someone is entering or leaving. When someone is entering, they get the Holy Ghost and then they must begin allowing the trimming process to take place. The pastor, the word, and the Holy Ghost all work together to trim away the world from the new saint. As they stay in the process, that old worldly light is extinguished and the Holy Ghost light becomes brighter. That is such an awesome and wonderful thing.

However, the same thing happens in reverse when someone is leaving the church. The Holy Ghost light is slowly extinguished in them as the light of the world gets brighter and brighter. If the process is not halted, they will eventually be out the church door and on their way to the world. Yet even though that worldly light is visible for a time as they step out the door, once they are gone the door closes back and the only light visible in the Holy Place is from the candlestick.

One problem with churches today is that they want to open the door and let the light of the world shine in. It is becoming too troublesome to many churches to keep the wick trimmed and the oil full. It is becoming too burdensome to teach holiness and separation.

Why go through the trouble when all you have to do is pull back the curtain and there is all the light that you will ever need. The light of their 'new revelations' have replaced the light of truth. Now it is no longer per God's pattern. It is now man's plan.

Yet let me point out some issues with pulling back the curtain and leaving it open. Sure, there is light that pours in and you can see. However, the light is not the only thing that pours in. There are things that enter with the light of the world that you cannot see with the naked eye. There are spirits that accompany that light which are destructive to the church body.

It is like those microorganisms that are being allowed to enter. Understand that the atmosphere is filled with innumerable microorganisms which we exist in every day. From my study of microbiology, I can testify that this is very real. You can take an agar plate of SBA (Sheep Blood Agar) and remove the lid and place it on your counter. You can return a few hours later and take that same plate, replace the lid, and then incubate it for 24 hours at 37 degrees Celsius. When you take that plate out of the incubator, it will be covered with numerous colonies of microorganisms.

No one must place these microorganisms on the plate, they settle there from the atmosphere around us. Although there is no Bible for it, I believe that the incense that was burned twice a day in the Tabernacle was antimicrobial in its action. I believe that it would have inhibited the growth of microorganisms. I base this on the fact that the Showbread was left on the Table of Shewbread for seven days before it was eaten.

This should have been impossible without some type of microbial growth inhibition. I am aware that God could have made this happen Himself, but I find it interesting that He provided the recipe for the incense and He charged the priest to make sure they followed that recipe. There was to be no strange incense burned there.

If this is the case, then the morning and evening burning of incense should have resulted in enough volume of incense to protect the Holy Place. The few visits to the Holy place would have been accompanied with the burning of incense. This would have created a cloud of incense that would have poured out the door when they left thereby ensuring that no organisms could enter.

Now you may ask what this has to do with anything. I'm glad you asked. For you see, when those that desire the light of world pull back the curtain and use that light, they are allowing all the incense to flow out and there is no longer any protection left inside the Holy Place. Now, the holy bread will be contaminated and corrupted by the microorganisms that will settle on it. The microorganisms only need a food source to thrive.

When this corruption of the bread (word) occurs, it becomes undesirable due to the microbial growth. Then the old bread gets thrown out and only the new bread is desired and consumed. However, understand that even the new bread must be changed quickly, else it too, become corrupt and undesirable. That is a problem of those leaving truth.

Their word (bread) is always changing and evolving. They can no longer keep teachings in place for long else it too become an offense to the people. So, they must continually change with the times and the desires of the people.

Once this occurs, you can be certain that the Courtyard Fence has long ago been dismantled. Now there is no longer just one entrance inside, but rather almost any entrance is accepted. Differences of doctrine become viewed as simply a difference in interpretation. Stands on holiness and separation depart with the fence. No longer can these fenceless churches be differentiated from the world. Over time they evolve to the place where they feel that everyone is going to be saved. If someone chooses to enter a different way, that is fine. They are all going to same place.

This is such a tragedy. Yet you can trace it all back to one of two things. Else they let their fence down or else they opened up the Holy Place to the light of the world. Whichever came first is not the point. Because if one of those things occurs, the other will definitely follow. Churches that are throwing teaching of holiness and separation from the world out the door, are already on the path described above.

Those churches that are embracing the teachings of this current generation over the teachings of the elders are also on that path. It doesn't matter if today is your first step in that direction on that path or if you have traveled miles down that path already. The thing is, you are all on the same path and that path leads to destruction. Get off that path NOW, and get back on the old paths and walk with Jesus.

Chapter 10

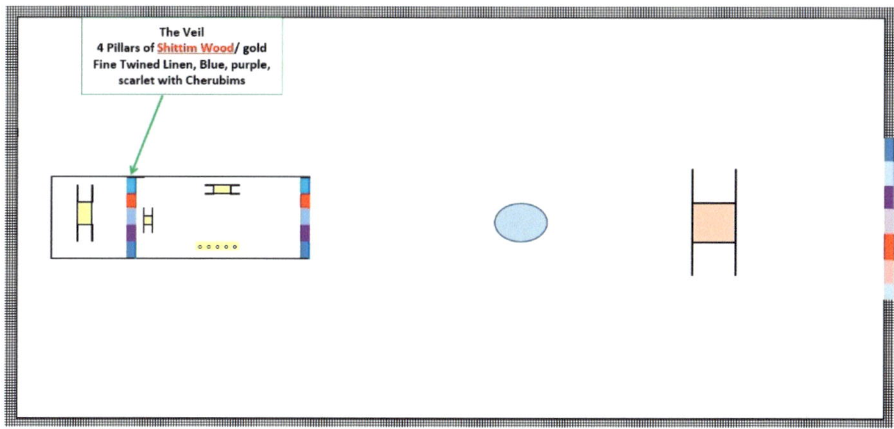

Figure 12- The Veil

Scriptures to study on the Veil:

Exodus 26: 31-33

Exodus 36: 8-19

The Veil was a curtain that separated the Holy Place from the Holy of Holies. It hung from four posts made of Shittim Wood overlaid with gold. It was composed of blue, purple, scarlet, and fine twined linen with Cheribims woven into it. It stretched from the south wall of the Holy Place to the north wall of the Holy Place.

The Veil was used to cover the Ark when the Tabernacle was moved. No one was to pass through the Veil except the high priest, and that was only on the Day of Atonement. This Veil is what hid the Ark, or the presence of God, from the people.

We find in ***Hebrews 10: 20*** that the flesh of Jesus was referred to as the Veil. With this in mind, look back at Calvary to where Jesus hung on the cross. It was there that He died and His flesh was rent by the soldier. At that exact moment, the Veil in the Temple was rent in twain from top to bottom according to ***Mark 15: 38***. I am sure that those priests that were in the Temple were shocked beyond description when that which had always been hidden was now revealed to all.

However, based upon study of the scripture, the Ark was lost to the Jews when they went into captivity. Therefore, whatever they had behind their Veil in this Temple was not the original Ark. I am sure that they all rushed forward to look behind this Veil that was rent to see what was there. However, what they really wanted to see was hanging on the cross.

That Veil of flesh of Jesus Christ hid the Mighty God within it. Just as it was in the Tabernacle, the presence of God was hidden behind a Veil so no one could see it. If one understands that the Ark was the visible representation of God in the Old Testament, then it is easy to see that Jesus Christ was also a type of the Ark. He was hidden from the Jews by a Veil over their eyes and His flesh was a Veil that hid the presence of God (***II Corinthians 3: 13-16***).

Therefore, when those priests ran forward to view the Ark behind the Veil of the Temple, that Ark was gone. The only visible Ark they could have seen was hanging on the cross of Calvary. Understand also that the ONLY people that even knew that the Veil was rent in the temple was the priesthood. No one else had access to the Holy Place except them.

Hebrews 10: 19-20 lets us know that we have access to the Holy of Holies by the blood of Jesus and the rending of His flesh. No one knows this today except the priesthood which is us (the saved) (***I Peter 2: 9***). The only way for the rest of the world to know that the Veil was rent in the Temple, was by the priests going out and telling them. The only way that the world will know that the Veil of Christ was rent for them is for the priesthood to go out and tell them. The world does not have access to the Holy Place. They must be born again of the water and spirit to be adopted into the priesthood (***John 3: 1-8, Ephesians 1: 4-5, Galatians 4: 4-5, Romans 8: 13-17***). Yet they must first know about it.

Chapter 11

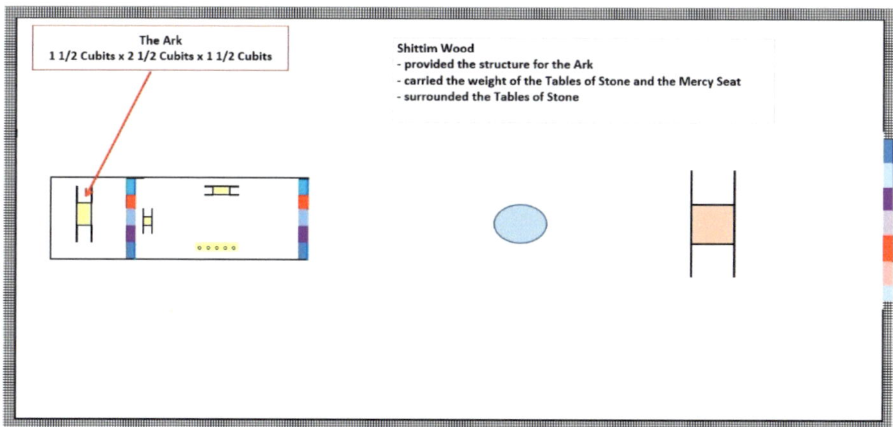

Figure 13- The Ark

Scriptures to study on the Ark:

Exodus 25: 10-16

Exodus 37: 1-5

The Ark was the only structure which resided behind the Veil in the Holy of Holies. There were not two or three Arks, but rather just one Ark, just as there but one God. The Ark measured one and a half cubits by two and a half cubits by one and a half cubits high. It had four rings which were set in each corner. It was made of Shittim Wood overlaid with pure gold.

There were two staves used to carry the Ark. These staves were made of Shittim Wood overlaid with gold. Once these staves were placed into the rings of the Ark, they were never to be removed according to the commandment of God. Within the Ark was the Tables given Moses (the Law), the pot of manna, and the Rod of Aaron that budded. Placed on top of the Ark as a lid was the Mercy Seat.

Once the Ark was placed inside the Tabernacle, no man was to ever see it again except for the high priest on the Day of Atonement. When the Ark was moved, it was carried on the shoulders of the priests by the staves and was covered by the Veil. The Ark could not be touched by anyone. The only way the priests could move the Ark, or interact with the Ark, was by using the staves.

The Ark represented the very presence of God. A study of the 'rings' reveals that the word used there was the same word used in ***Esther 3: 12*** when King Ahasuerus took off his 'ring' and allowed Haman to use it to seal the decrees. The use of the King's signet ring to seal a decree, or anything, gave the full authority and might of the King to whatever was written therein. In the book of Esther, we find that once something is sealed with the King's ring, it cannot be changed (***Esther 8: 8***).

Study of the staves in the original Hebrew reveals that the meaning of the word staves is actually 'separation' and 'branch'. The staves were used to separate man from physically touching the Ark. However, if you look at the other meaning, branch, then you can begin to link the staves to The Branch mentioned in ***Isaiah 4: 2, Isaiah 11: 1, Jeremiah 23: 5, Jeremiah 33: 15, Zechariah 3: 8,*** and ***Zechariah 6: 12***. That Branch is Jesus Christ.

The Shittim Wood is found throughout the Tabernacle. It is found in the Courtyard Fence posts, the Brazen Altar, the walls of the Tabernacle Proper, the Table of Showbread, the Altar of Incense, and the Ark. In some places, it was overlaid with gold, silver, brass, or simply exposed. In my study of the Tabernacle I concluded, through much prayer and study, and propose to you that the Shittim Wood represents separation and foundational truths, or the word.

Note that the Ark was overlaid with pure gold as was the Altar of Incense, and the Table of Shewbread. The other items, including the staves, were overlaid with gold (not PURE gold). During months of studying the Tabernacle and seeking God and His wisdom, a meaning for the pure gold was laid on my heart. The meaning provided ties everything else together in a beautiful picture.

I offer up that the pure gold represents the pure, sinless nature of God. There is no impurity in Him; He is perfect and pure. Notice that the Ark, which represents God's presence, is overlaid with pure gold. The Mercy Seat which sat on the Ark and was in physical contact with it was also made with pure gold. The Table of Showbread, which represented the Word of God, was overlaid with pure gold. ***Psalms 30: 5*** states that every word of God is pure. The Altar of Incense was overlaid with pure gold also. ***Exodus 37: 29*** indicates that the incense that was made was pure. Finally, the Candlestick was made from pure gold. ***Psalms 12: 6, Psalms 119: 140,*** and ***Proverbs 30: 5*** all state that the Word of the Lord is pure.

Looking at these meanings as a whole, a beautiful picture arises about the Ark. The Staves were overlaid with gold and slid into rings of gold which were attached to the Ark. Those staves represent the Branch, Jesus Christ, which housed the Living Word Incarnate within Him. Yet the man Christ Jesus was robed not in a glorified body, but rather, He was robed in flesh just like you and me.

Those staves were overlaid with just plain gold, which represents the sinless flesh of man. The flesh of man will never reach the purity of God; it is impossible. The closest we can come to purity is to be holy and separated unto God. Remember that holy and unholy or clean and unclean cannot intermingle. The flesh of man could never become holy enough to touch our holy God. However, when man is filled with the Holy Ghost, baptized in His name, and is living a repentant life doing all he can to be holy, God's grace makes up the difference.

It is by His grace that our flesh can approach and that we have access to the Holy of Holies. That golden ring on the Ark allowed the Staves to be attached to the pure gold. Those golden rings were like the grace of God that was attached to God on one side and man on the other.

Grace can be described as someone that is holding to a point of safety above while reaching down for someone trying to climb to safety up the side of a mountain. When you have climbed as high as you can go, grace comes to you and helps you the rest of the way. Thank God for His grace that enables man to be able to interact with our holy God.

Therefore, we have the staves (Jesus) being placed in the signet ring of the King. This is the ring that He used to stamp the new covenant, which is the New Testament salvation plan. It was stamped with the signet ring which held Jesus. This gospel that we have was purchased at Calvary and it was stamped with the blood of Jesus Christ. The commandment was that once those staves were placed in the ring they were to never be removed. When Jesus arrived, and purchased the church, He has remained in the signet. He is what we talk about, He is what we think about, He is who our hope is in, and He is the one whose return we are awaiting. When Jesus was stamped on this new covenant, He has remained and always will.

It is also interesting to note that when the Ark was moved, all that was visible to man were the staves and the Veil. The only visible part of the invisible God that man will ever see is Jesus Christ. He was the staves and His flesh was the Veil.

Also, understand that the only part of the Ark that could be touched or handled by man was the staves. They are what allowed man to move the Ark thereby guiding the camp to wherever God was taking them. Jesus is the mediator between man and God. He is at the right hand of God making intercession for us according to ***Romans 8: 34***.

When we get ahold of Jesus and hang on, He is able to lead us and guide us in the paths to salvation and eternal life. When man's hands are taken off Jesus, then there is no longer any movement toward where God is leading His people. The Ark can only be moved by holding onto Jesus.

Chapter 12

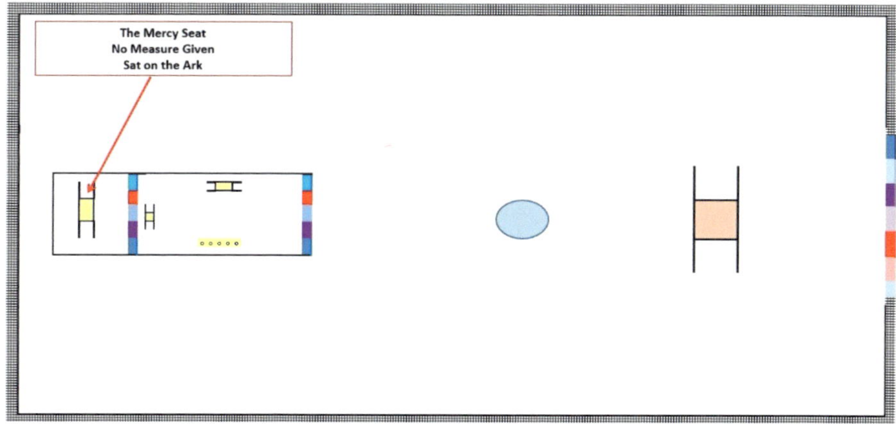

<u>Figure 14</u>- The Mercy Seat

Scriptures to study on the Mercy Seat:

Exodus 25: 17-22

Exodus 37: 6-9

The final structure in the Tabernacle is the Mercy Seat. This was a structure that sat on top of the Ark. It was made of <u>pure gold</u> two and a half cubits by one and a half cubits. However, its height is not given. It was a lid that had a Cherubim of gold on one end of it and a Cherubim of gold on the other end of it. These Cherubims faced each other and had wings that were stretched forth on high covering the Mercy Seat. The area under their wings, which they were facing, is where God told Moses that He would meet with him and commune with him.

Romans 3: 25 speaks of God setting forth Christ Jesus to be a propitiation for the remission of sins. Looking at the word propitiation in the original Greek, it is found that it occurs only twice in the New Testament. The other occurrence is in ***Hebrews 9: 5*** where it means the Mercy Seat.

Therefore, looking back at ***Romans 3: 25*** we can clearly see that Jesus has become our Mercy Seat. It was by His sacrifice at Calvary that we have remission of sins through His blood. This was not the blood of bulls and goats, but was rather the precious blood of the Lamb of God. It is by the sacrifice of that spotless Lamb that we have mercy with God. It is in Jesus Christ that we meet with, and commune with, God. Jesus has truly become our Mercy Seat.

Based on this, we can make the following determinations about Jesus Christ:

- Jesus is the Scapegoat. He took all our sins upon Himself.
- Jesus is the Fit Man. He took those sins and carried them so far away that they can never return to the camp, or to us.
- Jesus is the Sacrifice. He is the Lamb that was sacrificed from the foundation of the world. He was offered so that we might have eternal life.

- Jesus is the name used in baptism. It is the blood of the sacrifice that is in the water of the Laver. Jesus is the Sacrifice; therefore, it is the blood of Jesus that is in baptism for remission of sins.
- Jesus is the High Priest. He offered Himself a sacrifice for our sins.
- Jesus is the Candlestick. He is the Light of the world.
- Jesus is the Showbread. He is that bread that came down from heaven.
- Jesus is the Incense. He is the one that we pray to and we worship.
- Jesus is the Veil. It is through the rending of His body (Veil) at Calvary that we have access into the Holy of Holies.
- Jesus is the Staves. He is the only visible part of the invisible God that man will ever see. It is Him that we reach for and hold on to when we need to touch God.
- Jesus is the Mercy Seat. We obtain mercy through His blood and He has become our Mercy Seat.
- Jesus is the Ark. God was manifest in the flesh. That means He was made VISIBLE in the flesh. This was in the man Christ Jesus. ***Colossians 1: 15-16*** says that Jesus is the image of the invisible God.

The Tabernacle points toward Jesus in such a beautiful way. When you know who Jesus is, it is easy to put all the pieces together.

Note, for mercy to be extended to the camp of Israel, there had to first be blood applied to the Mercy Seat on the Day of Atonement. For us to receive mercy today, we must have the spotless blood of Jesus applied to the Mercy Seat. To do this you must bring yourself as a sacrifice to the Altar of repentance (the Brazen Altar). There you offer yourself in godly sorrow for the sins that you have committed. However, when you are ready to lay down your life for your transgressions, you find that another has already died for your sins.

Now you can get up from the Altar of repentance knowing that you have been forgiven of your sins. You must understand at this point, however, that you still have judgment against you for previous sins. The violation of God's law, the Bible, carries with it a penalty that is not erased at the Altar of repentance.

Think of the modern legal system. If you murder someone and are caught by the authorities. The family of that person that you murdered may forgive you for what that have done. Everyone may be stirred to compassion and forgive you of the murder. However, the law has some stipulations that must be met even though you were forgiven. You must stand before a judge and receive your sentence for the crime you committed. You may get prison or you may get the death penalty. Either way, you must pay for the crime.

That is how it is in the Kingdom of God. You receive forgiveness when you repent, but you still owe a debt that must be paid. That debt is to be paid at the White Throne of Judgment. So, what do we do?

If you look at the Tabernacle, once you enter the Tabernacle you stop first at the Brazen Altar. This is where you repent. When you leave there, the next thing you come to is the Brazen Laver. This is baptism. You must wash in the Laver before you go any farther else you die. Remember that the blood of the sacrifice (Jesus) is in the water. When you are baptized in the name of Jesus Christ for the remission of sins, you are having the blood of the Lamb applied. Calling the name of Jesus in baptism puts the blood in the water.

According to the concordance, remission carries the following meanings:

- Release from bondage or imprisonment
- Forgiveness or pardon of sins
- Letting them go as if they had never been committed
- Remission of the penalty

Now the importance of baptism becomes so much clearer. When you are baptized in the name of Jesus Christ for the remission of sins (as ***Acts 2: 38*** states), you are having your penalty removed. You obtain a pardon. It is looked at as though you never even sinned at all. In essence, your sins are taking from you and sent ahead to judgment where they are deemed as pardoned by the blood. They are erased and not remembered again.

Once you have repented and received a pardon for your sins at the Laver, you are ready to enter the Holy Place. When you enter the Holy Place, you step into a place where the lighting changes. No longer are you seeing by the light of the world but rather by the light of Jesus Christ. The light of revelation is shining in your life.

That light shines on the Showbread (the Word of God) and allows you see it "in a new light". Now when you read the Bible there is new revelation that is revealed due to your experience at the Altar and the Laver. You are drawn to the Altar of Incense (prayer and worship) as others begin to offer incense. You come to enjoy the sweet aroma of worship and prayer and begin to offer up your own.

The final thing for you to visit is the Ark. This was prohibited to all but the High Priest until Calvary. Then our High Priest made a way for us all to go boldly through the Veil to the Throne of Grace (***Hebrews 4: 16***). Entering the Holy of Holies places you directly into the presence of God. This is the realm of the supernatural. It is here we recognize the greatness of our God and the weakness of ourselves. This is where you truly offer yourself to God as you lift Him up and worship Him humbly from the heart. When you reach the point where you fully understand God's might and fully surrender your will to His will, then you will receive the Holy Ghost.

Understand that there are many people that do not understand the things of God. They truly do not understand the meaning of the Tabernacle or God's plan of salvation. These people argue that you do not need the Holy Ghost, you do not need to be baptized in Jesus name, and you do not need to repent. Some even go so far as to say that there is no need to separate the holy from the unholy and the clean from the unclean. They think for some reason that God has changed and that now He embraces the unclean and unholy mixing them in with the pure and calling it all pure.

The Bible states that God never changes (***Hebrews 13:8***). Why would man think that God, who put so much emphasis and effort into making sure that holy and unholy never intermingled and that clean and unclean never intermingled, would suddenly change His mind? Why would this holy God choose to change to become an unholy God? God did not create a plan to save man in which He would debase Himself so that man could continue in His sins. No, God created a plan where man could come OUT of his sins and be holy like his God.

I Peter 1:16 says "be ye holy; for I am holy". God was still shouting that He was holy even when the apostles were preaching and the church had started. He had not gone out of the holiness business. No, He sent Peter to tell the people, YOU get holy for I am holy. He is not going to allow the holy and unholy to mix even today.

In other words, YOU MUST receive the Holy Ghost. According to ***John 3: 1-8*** you must be born again of the water and the spirit to see heaven or to enter heaven. You really do not get a full revelation of heaven or the Kingdom of God until you receive the Holy Ghost. To forbid the Holy Ghost requires you to throw away the Tabernacle. You must ignore any spiritual meaning from the scriptures and just view them as just history alone.

I am sorry. The Bible is the inspired word of God and it was not penned just for history. It is a living word that sheds light on how to live righteously and be saved even to this day. In the catching away of the Church it is the Lord calling His spirit (the Holy Ghost) out of the world that we await. It is the Holy Ghost being called out of this old world that is going to open the way for the Tribulation spoken of in the book of Revelations. If you have the Holy Ghost, then you are going to be "caught away". If you do not have the Holy Ghost, then there will be no "catching away" for you.

Appendix of Figures

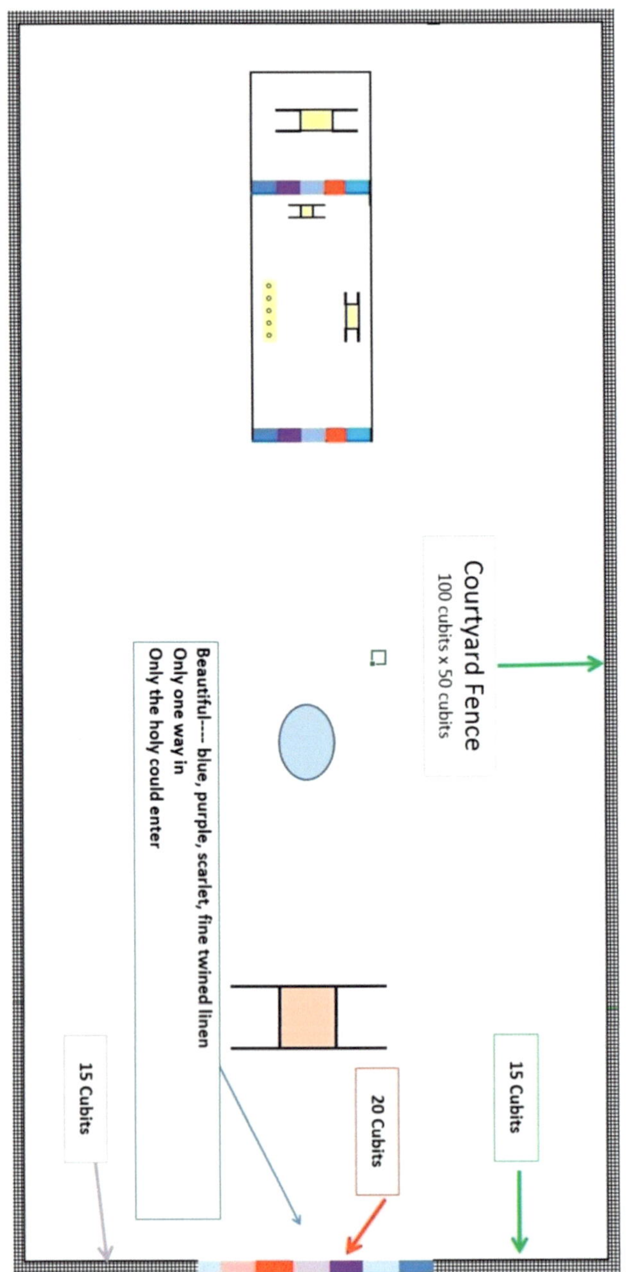

Figure 2

The Courtyard Fence

Figure 3

Arrangement of the Camp of Israel

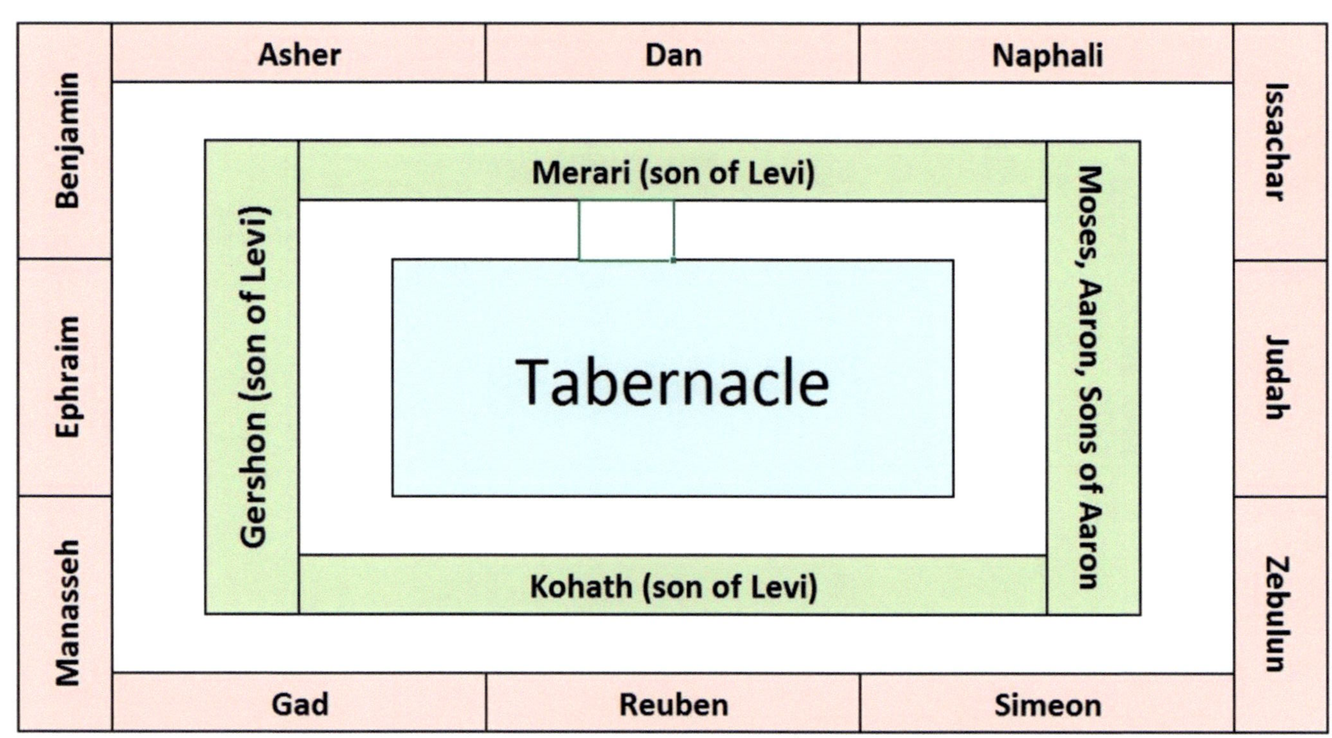

Figure 4

The Courtyard Fence

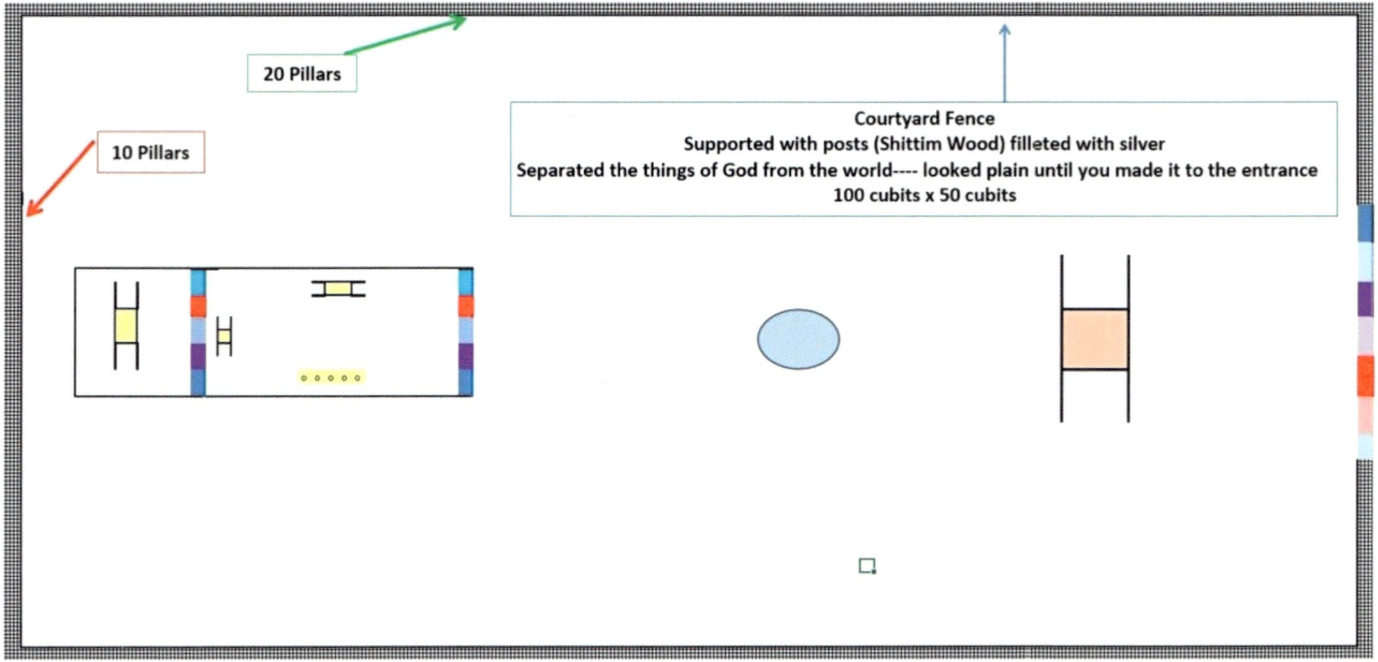

20 Pillars

10 Pillars

Courtyard Fence
Supported with posts (Shittim Wood) filleted with silver
Separated the things of God from the world---- looked plain until you made it to the entrance
100 cubits x 50 cubits

Figure 5

The Tabernacle without the Courtyard Fence

(The Church of Today- No Separation)

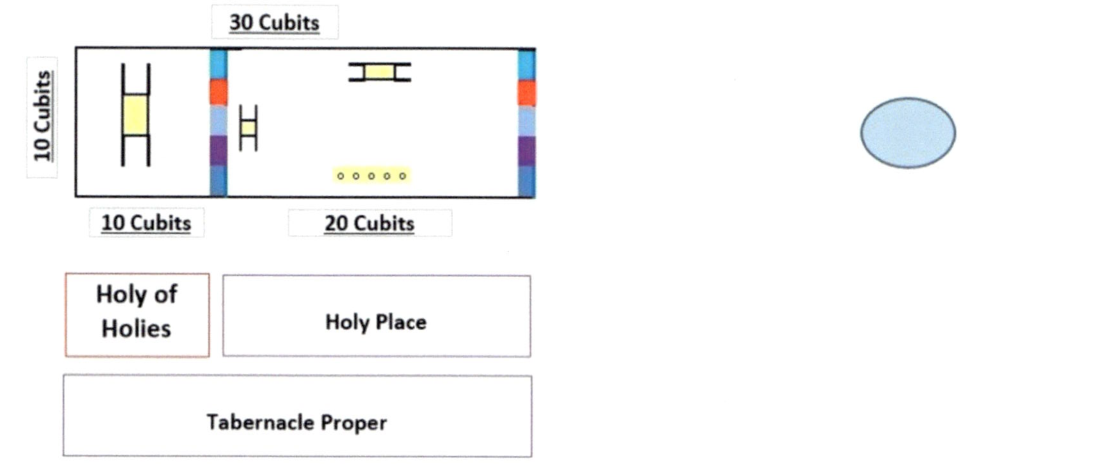

Figure 6

The Brazen Altar

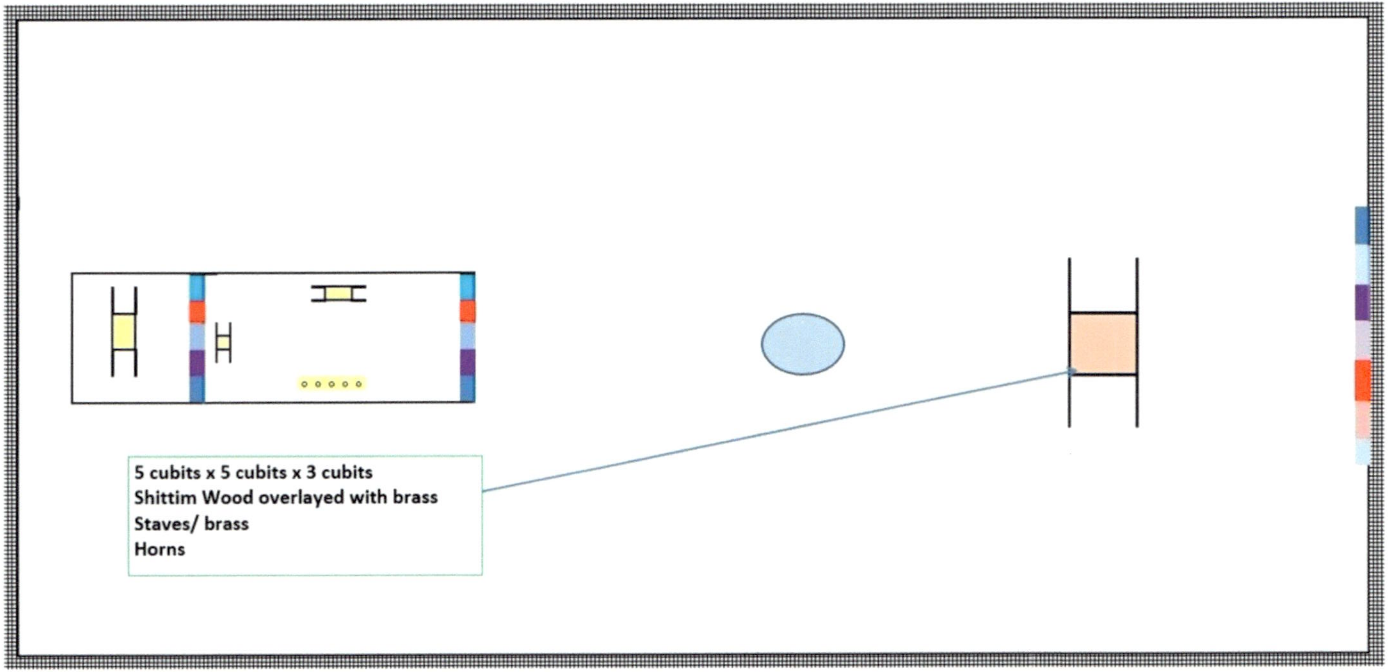

Figure 7

The Brazen Laver

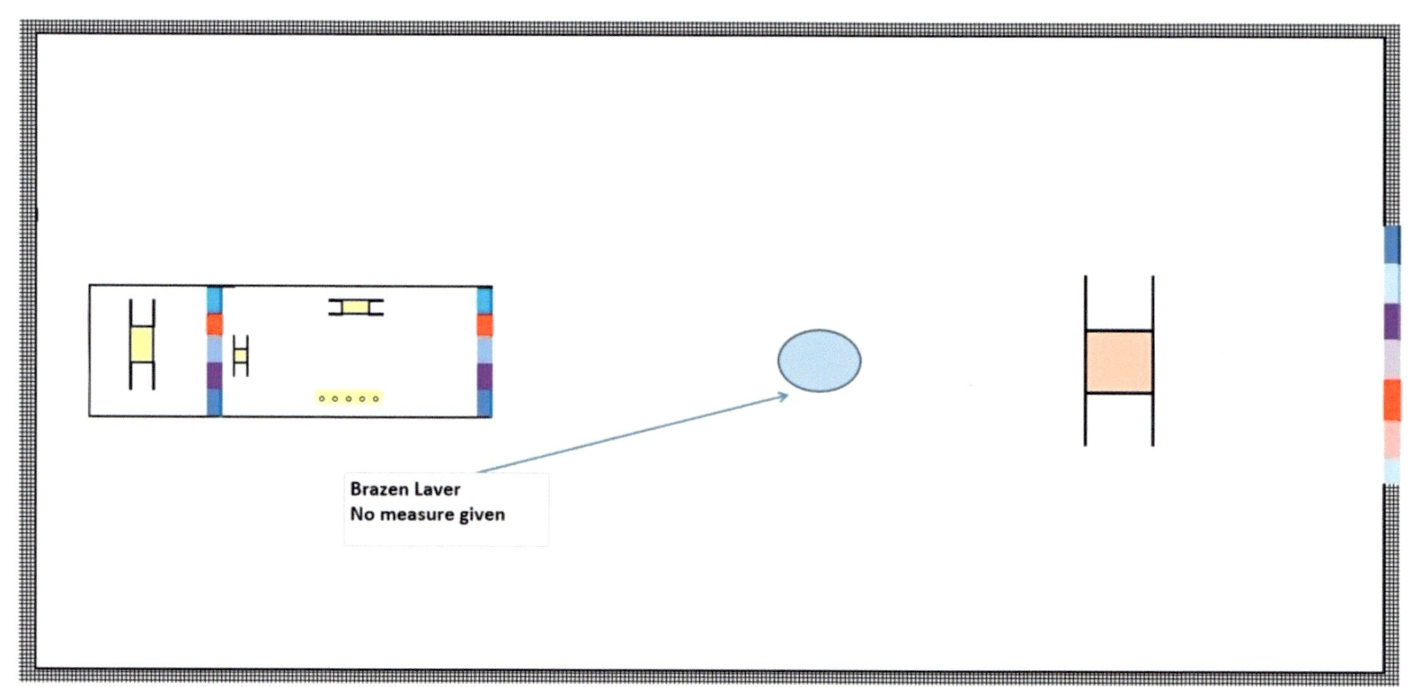

Figure 8

The Tabernacle Proper

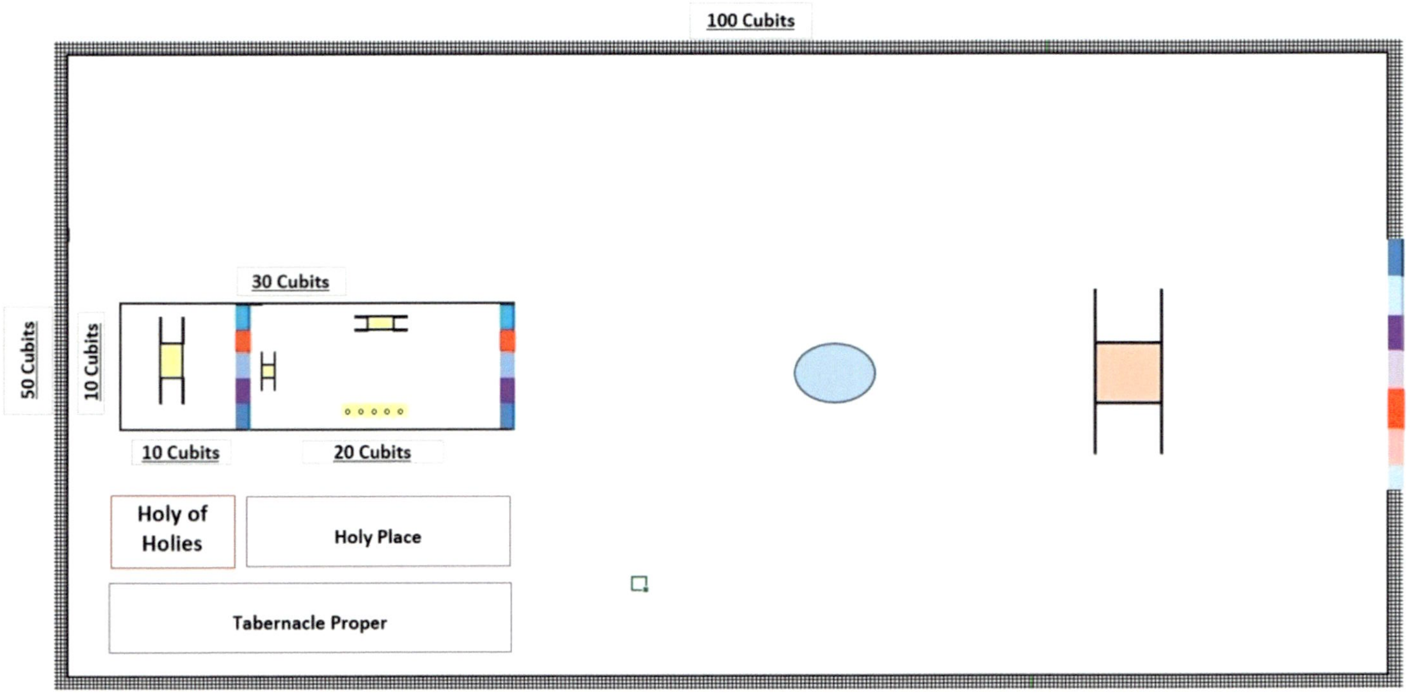

100 Cubits

50 Cubits

30 Cubits

10 Cubits

10 Cubits

20 Cubits

Holy of Holies

Holy Place

Tabernacle Proper

Figure 9

The Table of Shewbread

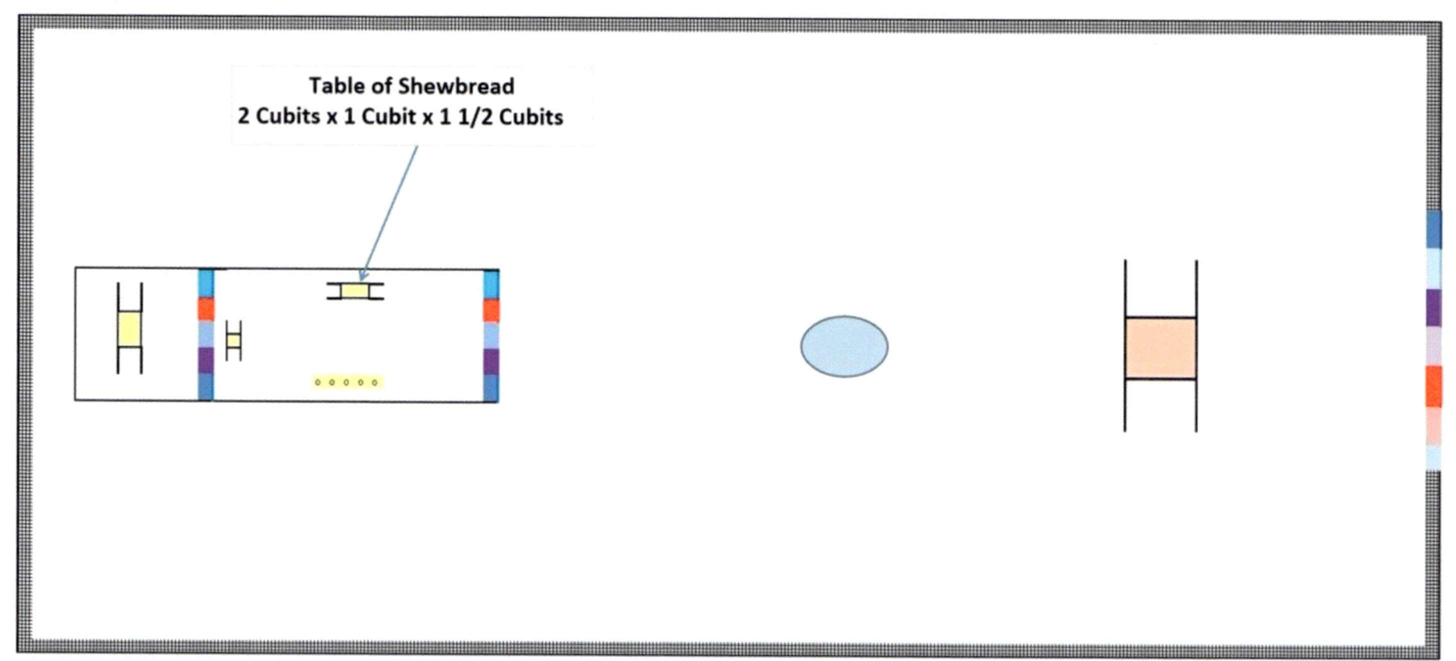

Figure 10

The Altar of Incense

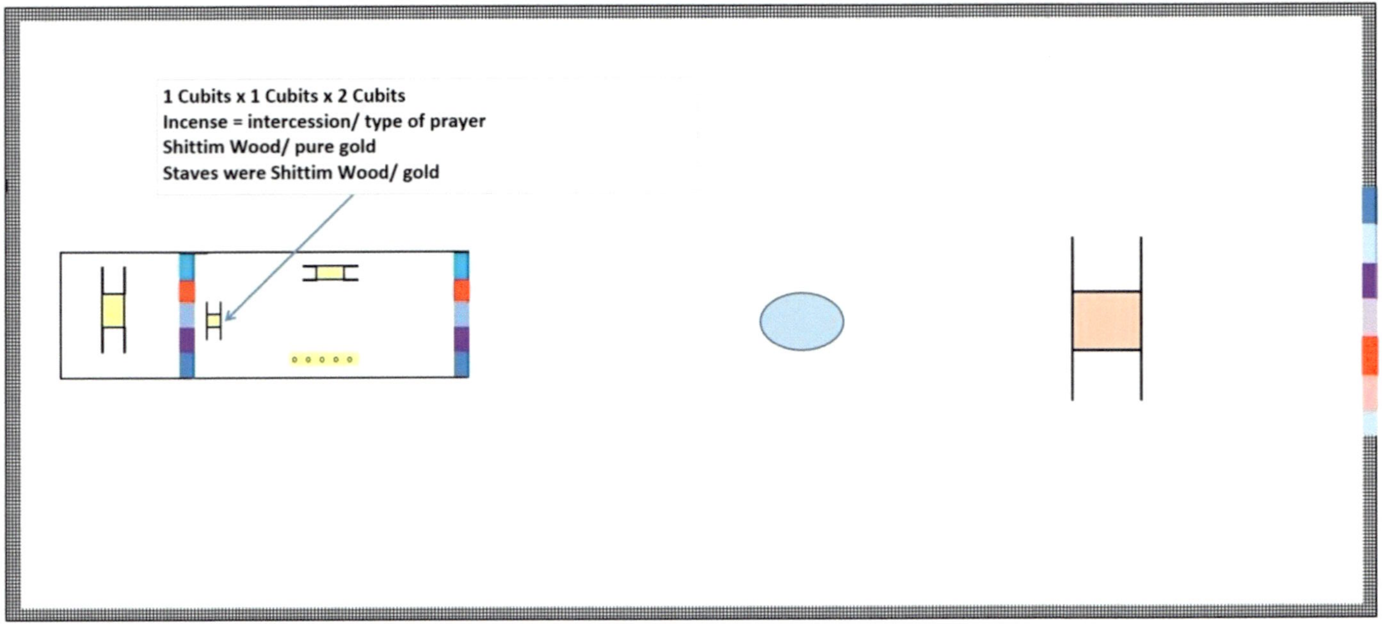

1 Cubits x 1 Cubits x 2 Cubits
Incense = intercession/ type of prayer
Shittim Wood/ pure gold
Staves were Shittim Wood/ gold

Figure 11

The Candlestick

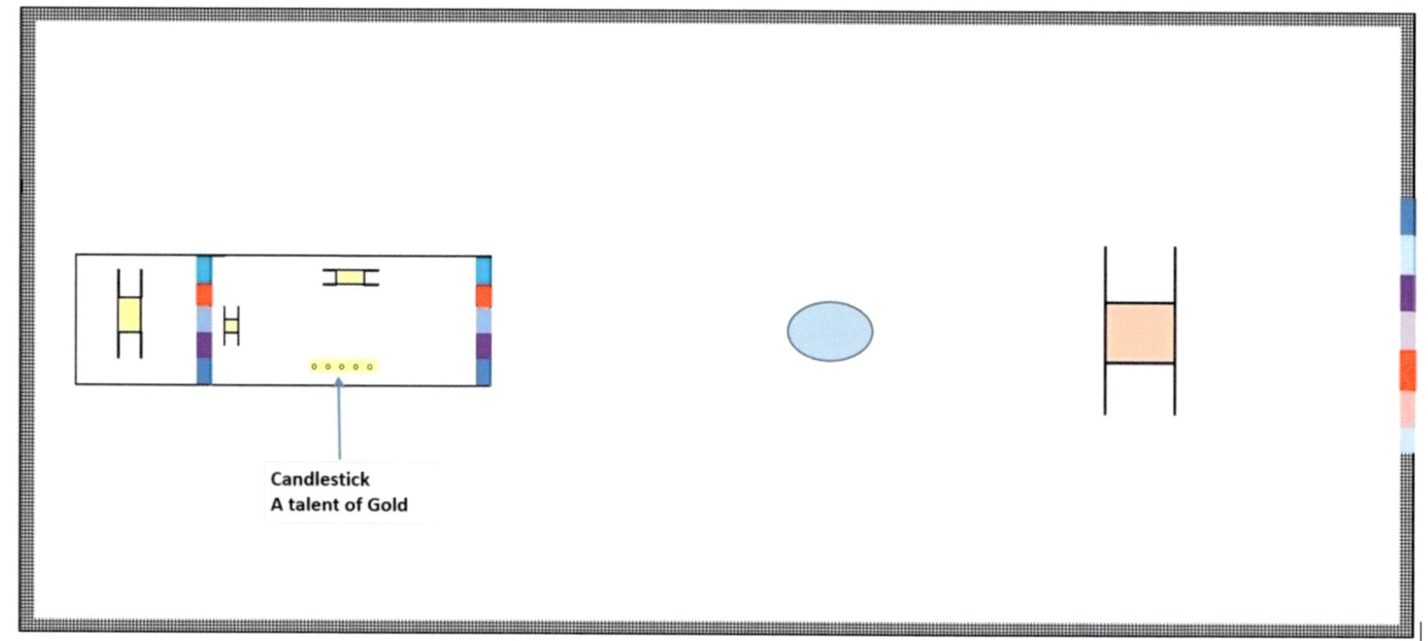

Figure 12

The Veil

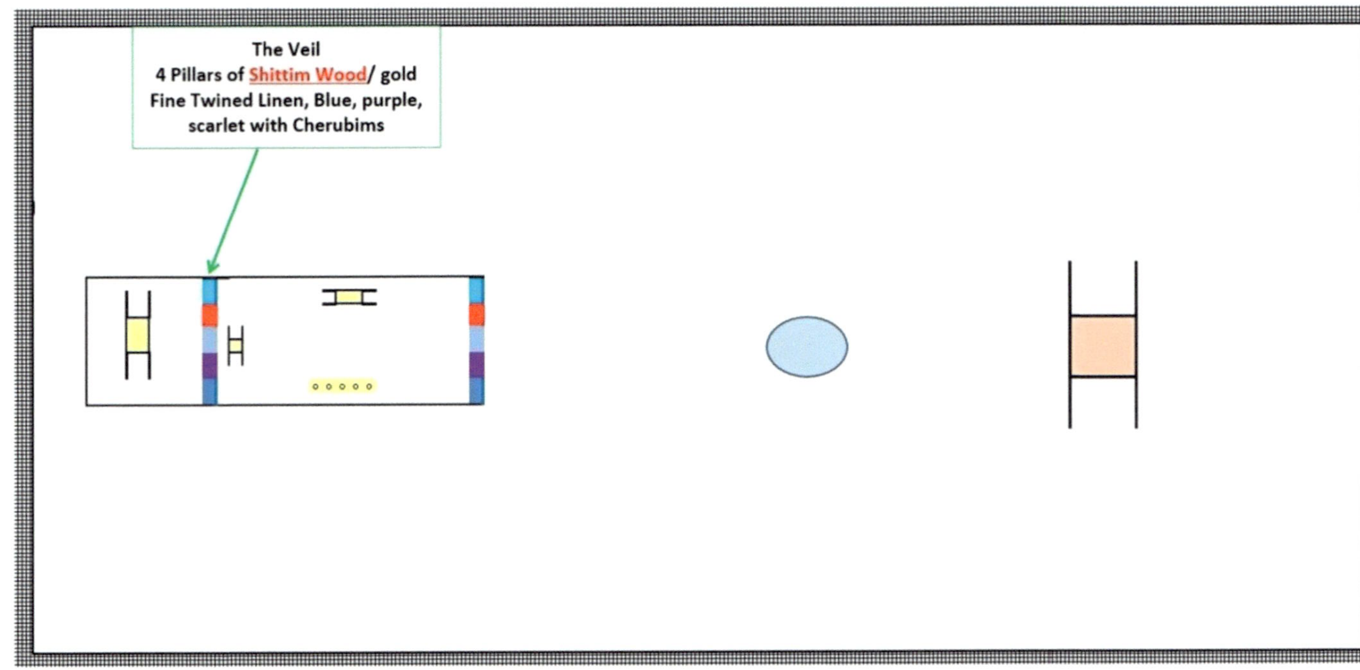

Figure 13

The Ark

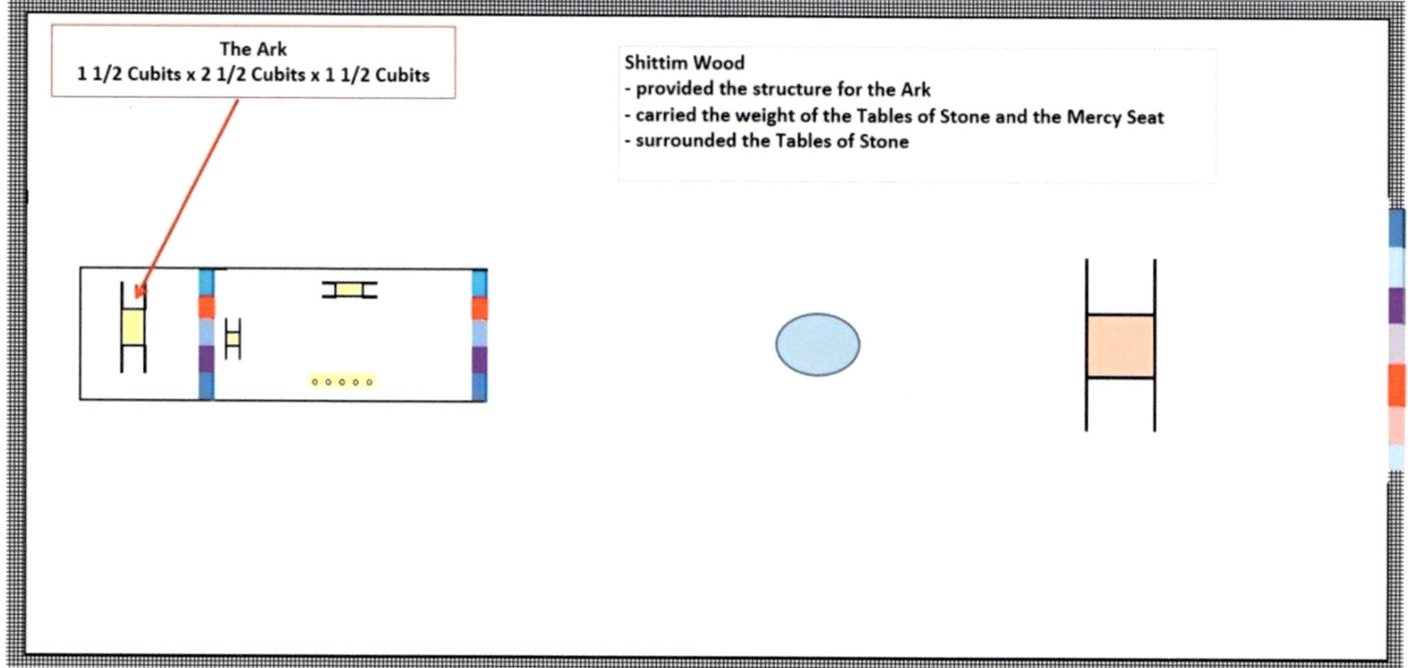

Figure 14

The Mercy Seat

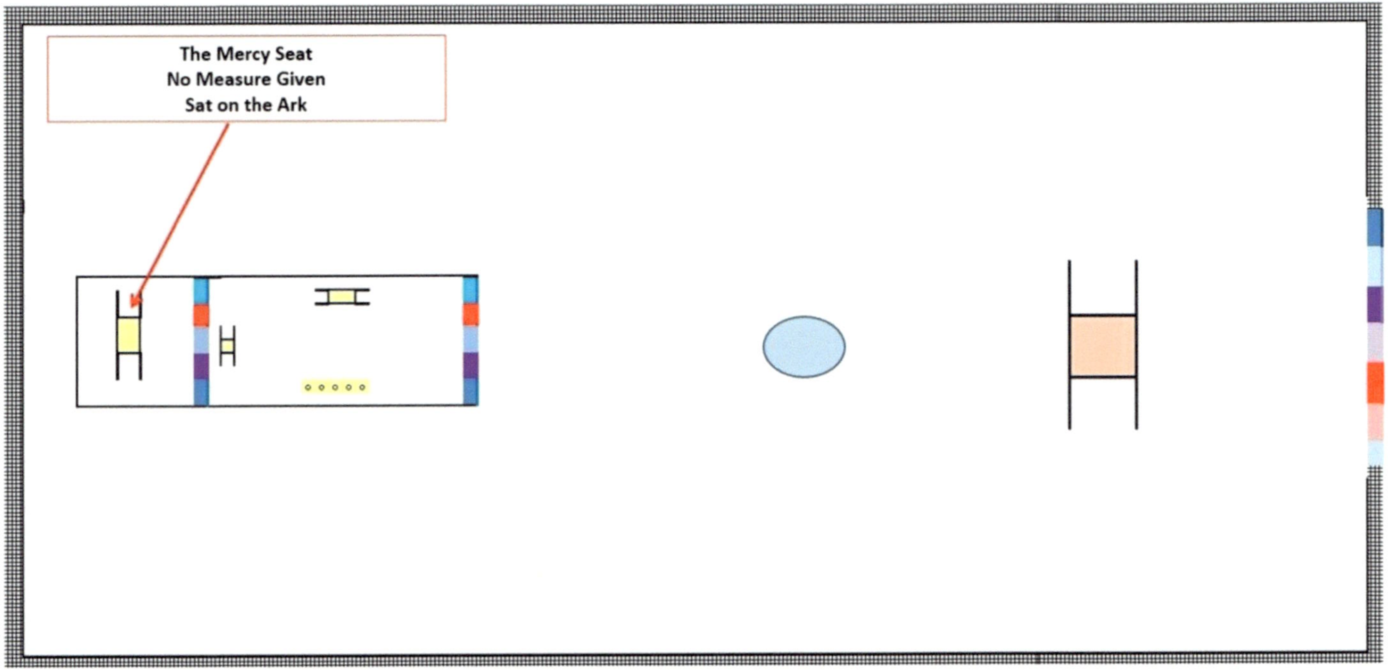

The Mercy Seat
No Measure Given
Sat on the Ark

About the Author

The author is married and has three children and soon to be four grandchildren. He was not raised as an Apostolic Pentecostal, but was rather a Trinitarian. He came to the knowledge of the Truth in 1998 when he was baptized in the name of Jesus Christ for the remission of his sins, and then he received the Holy Ghost as evidenced by speaking in tongues as the Spirit gave the utterance.

This Holy Ghost experience caused the author to abandon his old way of life and to start seeking the Lord and the Lord's way. Years of sitting under a great Bible teacher and studying the Word of God led to the Holy Ghost moving upon the author to write down some of the things he was learning.

The author hopes and prays that these books can be a resource to help point others toward researching the Word and God and seeking His holy and righteous ways. With the ease of publishing a book today, God fearing people should humble themselves and seek to publish what God lays on their hearts. There is a lost, dying, and hurting world out there that needs salvation, comfort, strength, and direction. God's people can be used to do this by allowing God to use you in the field of writing.

Other books by Wayne Spence

The Gospel's Sake is a look at the drinking of wine and whether it is acceptable to the Apostolic Pentecostal saint. This book looks at secular research on the issue with resources listed in the index for those that might wish to use this information themselves. There is also a biblical look at the issue of drinking wine and conclusions drawn from both the biblical and secular research. This work can also be found on **Amazon.com**.

Who's Watching the Master's Sheep looks at what appears to be an emerging trend in which some pastors are turning all their attention to reaching the lost. This trend is leading to departure of teaching godly principles of the Bible to the church and instead utilizing evangelistic preaching only. The book goes on to compare the results of the "Starvation Experiment" of World War II to the current church. The effects on the participants of this experiment are paralleled to the saints of churches that are abandoning teaching. It is a must read for all pastors and ministers for sure as well as to the saints that are struggling with these issues. This work can also be found on **Amazon.com**.

The Flower Comes Before the Fruit is a book that explores the trials, tribulations, and heart aches that can come to a saint of God. Life's circumstances can propel anyone into what the author calls "The World of Pain". Some of the reasons for the trails of life are explored along with how God views them many times. The process that God places the saints in is outlined along with suggestions on how to find God's will and stay in it. This book is a great resource for those that feel as though they are struggling with the storms of life and feel like just giving up. This work can also be found on **Amazon.com**.

Made in the USA
Columbia, SC
19 July 2025